Workbook

WORLD ENGLISH 3

SECOND EDITION

Real People • Real Places • Real Language

Kristin L. Johannsen, Author
Rob Jenkins, Series Editor

NATIONAL GEOGRAPHIC LEARNING | CENGAGE Learning

Australia • Brazil • Japan • Korea • Mexico • Singapore • Spain • United Kingdom • United States

NATIONAL GEOGRAPHIC LEARNING | CENGAGE Learning

World English Level 3 Workbook
Real People, Real Places, Real Language
Kristin L. Johannsen, Author
Rob Jenkins, Series Editor

Publisher: Sherrise Roehr

Executive Editor: Sarah Kenney

Senior Development Editor: Margarita Matte

Development Editor: Brenden Layte

Assistant Editor: Alison Bruno

Editorial Assistant: Patricia Giunta

Media Researcher: Leila Hishmeh

Senior Technology Product Manager: Scott Rule

Director of Global Marketing: Ian Martin

Senior Product Marketing Manager: Caitlin Thomas

Senior Director of ELT Production: Michael Burggren

Production Manager: Daisy Sosa

Content Project Manager: Andrea Bobotas

Senior Print Buyer: Mary Beth Hennebury

Cover Designer: Aaron Opie

Art Director: Scott Baker

Creative Director: Chris Roy

Cover Image: ©Manuel Higuera

Compositor: MPS Limited

Cover Image

Moroccan market: A quiet day at a souq in Morocco

World English 3 Workbook ISBN: 978-1-285-84845-7

National Geographic Learning
20 Channel Center Street
Boston, MA 02210
USA

Cengage Learning is a leading provider of customized learning solutions with office locations around the globe, including Singapore, the United Kingdom, Austrailia, Mexico, Brazil, and Japan.

Cengage Learning products are represented in Canada by Nelson Education, Ltd.

Visit National Geographic Learning online at ngl.cengage.com

Visit our corporate website at www.cengage.com

Printed in the United States of America
Print Number: 04 Print Year: 2018

CONTENTS

STUDENT BOOK SCOPE AND SEQUENCE

	Unit Goals	Grammar	Vocabulary
UNIT 1 **People and Places** Page 2 	• Discuss reasons for living where you do • Explain why you plan stay or leave • Describe a new place • Describe the city where you live	Present perfect tense vs. present continuous tense ***She has moved*** *three times in her life.* ***It's been raining*** *all day.* *So* + adjective + *that* *It's* ***so*** *dry here* ***that*** *water is brought in on trucks.*	Migration Climate
UNIT 2 **The Mind** Page 14 	• Talk about learning strategies • Talk about your senses • Talk about your fears • Describe an emotional experience	Gerunds as subjects and after prepositions ***Learning*** *English is important.* ***We*** *talked about* ***studying*** *together.* *May, might,* and *could* for possibility *We* ***may*** *find dangerous animals in the jungle.*	Thought processes Scientific studies
UNIT 3 **Changing Planet** Page 26 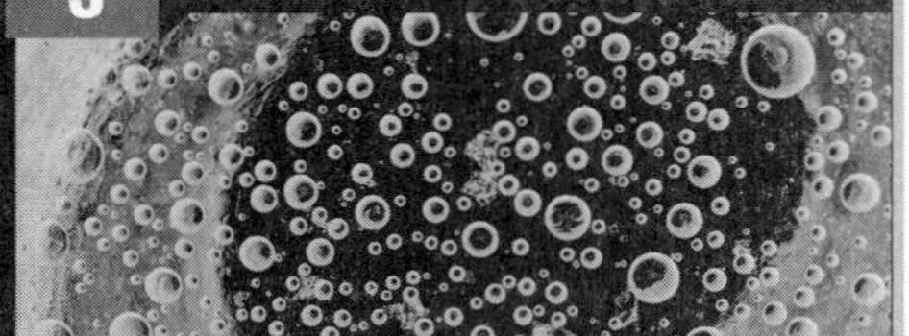	• Suggest solutions to environmental problems • Discuss causes and effects • Talk about invasive species • Discuss effects on the future	The passive—all tenses *Often, trees* ***are removed*** *to make room for farming.* The past perfect *By the time sea level* ***had risen*** *ten feet…*	Environmental changes Large numbers
TEDTALKS Video Page 38 **Paul Nicklen: Tales of Ice-bound Wonderlands**			
UNIT 4 **Money vs. Wealth** Page 42 	• Describe your financial habits • Discuss things that people value • Talk about banking • Talk about different types of wealth	Gerund vs. infinitive *I* ***try to make*** *a budget. /* ***I enjoy finding*** *bargains.* Review of the passive voice *Coffee* ***is grown*** *in Brazil.* *That movie* ***was made*** *by two teenagers.*	Money transactions Banking
UNIT 5 **Survival** Page 54 	• Talk about emergency situations • Evaluate survival methods • Describe how animals survive • Write a Brochure	Unreal conditional in the present *If they* ***weren't*** *inside the shelter, they* ***would*** *quickly* ***die****.* *Wish* in the present *I* ***wish*** *I had* ***brought*** *a good book to read in the shelter.*	Survival skills Environmental conservation
UNIT 6 **Art** Page 66 	• Report what another person said • Express your opinions about a piece of art • Describe your favorite artists and their art • Talk about public art	Reported speech ***She said she was tired and her head hurt.*** Subject adjective clauses *An artist* ***who works with clay has strong hands.***	Art Art materials
TEDTALKS Video Page 78 **Amit Sood: Building a Museum of Museums on the Web**			

Listening	Speaking and Pronunciation	Reading	Writing	Video Journal
Focused listening Interviews about why people live where they do	Discussing reasons for staying or moving Contractions with *have* and *be*	**National Geographic:** "Pioneers of the Pacific"	Writing a paragraph about a city	**National Geographic:** "San Francisco's Mission District"
Listening for general understanding and specific information A radio program about the unusual condition of synesthesia	Talking about sensations *Th* sounds	**National Geographic:** "In Your Face"	Writing about a personal experience	**National Geographic:** "Memory Man"
General and focused listening Climate change	Discussing cause and effect Linking words together	**TED**TALKS "Salvation (and Profit) in Greentech"	Writing a news article	**National Geographic:** "The Netherlands: Rising Water"
General and focused listening Radio program: The history of money	Giving suggestions for how to have fun for free Reduction of *to*	**TED**TALKS "Music is Medicine, Music is Sanity"	Writing a paragraph about valued things	**National Geographic:** "Making a Deal"
Listening for general understanding A radio program interviewing survivors	Simulation: working with a team in a survival situation Reduced sounds: *d'ya* and *didja*	**National Geographic:** "Survival School"	Writing an advertising brochure	**National Geographic:** "Andean Weavers"
Listening for general understanding Conversations in a museum	Discussing personal selections Thought groups	**National Geographic:** "Saving a City's Public Art"	Writing a detailed description	**National Geographic:** "Faces of India"

	Unit Goals	Grammar	Vocabulary
 	• Talk about new developments • Discuss choices in transportation • Use English to get around • Make recommendations for improving transportation	Passive voice with the present continuous and present perfect tenses *The new* ***plane is being tested*** *now. /Computers* ***have been used*** *for more than 50 years.* Indirect questions *Do you know* ***if the bus stops*** *here?*	Modern transportation Public transportation
 	• Talk about sports • Explain which sport is best for you • Talk about positive and negative aspects of competition • Discuss competitive advantages	Negative questions ***Don't*** *you want to go downtown with us?* Adjective clauses with object pronouns *The medal* ***that he won*** *was made of gold.*	Sportsmanship Sports
 	• Discuss ways to stay safe • Talk about dangerous work • Discuss personal emergencies • Discuss dangerous situations	Tag questions *Those spiders are poisonous,* ***aren't they?*** Adverbial clauses of time *I finished my project* ***before*** *I went home.*	Dangerous things Expressions for emergencies
 	• Speculate about mysteries • Discuss types of mysteries • Talk about plans you used to have • Explain a mysterious image	Modals for speculating about the past *He* ***might have seen*** *a large fish instead of a sea monster.* The future in the past *The two sisters* ***were going*** *to have a picnic by the lake.*	Ancient mysteries Reactions to surprise
 	• Talk about educational choices • Discuss your learning style • Talk about choosing a university major • Propose a new approach to teaching	*Should have, Would have, Could have* *I* ***should have applied*** *for a scholarship.* Noun clauses *I don't know* ***when the deadline is.***	Education University majors
 	• Talk about the future • Talk about life in space • Speculate about the future • Summarize a sequence of events	Talking about the future *Space exploration* ***will/is going to*** *be even more international in the future.* Modals and modal-like phrases to talk about the future ***We'll be able to*** *see it from here.*	Space exploration Future time expressions

Listening	Speaking and Pronunciation	Reading	Writing	Video Journal
Focused listening A discussion: Subway systems	Role-play: solving an airport problem Reduced *are*	**National Geographic:** "The Rickshaws of Kolkata"	Writing a letter to the editor of a newspaper	**National Geographic:** "Big City Bicycle Messengers"
Listening for general understanding and specific information Sports interviews	Matching sports to personalities Intonation to show surprise	**National Geographic:** "In Sports, Red is the Winning Color"	Writing a list of competition tips	**National Geographic:** "Women in The Rodeo"
Focused and general listening Radio program: An unusual job	Role-play: a newspaper interview Intonation of tag questions	**TED**TALKS "Three Things I Learned While My Plane Crashed"	Writing about emergency preparations	**National Geographic:** "Destroyers"
Listening for general understanding Interview of sea monster expert	Discussing different types of mysteries Intonation: Finished and unfinished ideas	**National Geographic:** "Hands Across Time"	Writing a comparison	**National Geographic:** "Crop Circles"
Listening for general understanding Learning experiences	Discussing quiz results Past modals	**TED**TALKS "Five Dangerous Things (You Should Let Your Children Do)"	Writing about new approaches to teaching	**National Geographic:** "Butler School"
General and focused listening Interview of an astronaut	Role-play: Choosing a space experiment Stress in compound nouns	**National Geographic:** "The Hubble Space Telescope"	Writing about space exploration	**National Geographic:** "Daring Mighty Things: Curiosity Lands on Mars"

CREDITS

ILLUSTRATION

65: (l, lm, rm, r) Keith Neely/IllustrationOnline.com; **73:** (t) National Geographic Maps.

PHOTOS

Cover Photo: Courtesy Manuel de la Higuera

9: (tr) Dunca Daniel/Hemera/Getty Images; **9:** (br) © iStock.com/Foremniakowski; **10:** (t) © iStock.com/Zurijeta; **10:** (m) O. LOUIS MAZZATENTA/National Geographic Creative; **10:** (b) © iStock.com/nycshooter; **11:** (c) jean-luc cochonneau/Alamy; **12:** (l) Photononstop/Photononstop; **12:** (r) Mattias Klum/ National Geographic Creative; **13:** (mr) Down Under Digital/Alamy; **15:** (t) XPACIFICA/National Geographic Creative; **15:** (b) © Stephen Coburn/Shutterstock.com; **16:** (r) © Victor Shova/Shutterstock.com; **16:** (l) © iStock.com/VLIET; **17:** (t) © iStock.com/Drbouz; **17:** (b) © Goodluz/Shutterstock.com; **18:** (t) © iStock.com/mediaphotos; **18:** (ml) © Diego Cervo/Shutterstock.com; **18:** (mr) © RyFlip/Shutterstock.com; **18:** (b) © iStock.com/laflor; **19:** (mr) Ray Fisher/The LIFE Images Collection/Getty Images; **21:** (tr) Woods Wheatcroft/Aurora+/Getty Images; **21:** (b) © Alexander Raths/Shutterstock.com; **22:** (tl) © iStock.com/Meinzahn; **22:** (t/m/l) © Yellowj/Shutterstock.com; **22:** (t/m/l) © Olaf Naami/Shutterstock.com; **22:** (t/m/r) © Nightman1965/Shutterstock.com; **22:** (tr) © iStock.com/RicAguiar; **23:** (t) © GuoZhongHua/Shutterstock.com; **24:** (t) © iStock.com/tinabelle; **24:** (m) © iStock.com/martiapunts; **24:** (b) © Cameron Whitman/Shutterstock.com; **25:** (t) © Elena Elisseeva/Shutterstock.com; **27:** (mr) © wavebreakmedia/Shutterstock.com; **27:** (b) AID/a.collectionRF/Getty Images; **28:** (tl) © Rtimages/Shutterstock.com; **29:** (t) © GWImages/Shutterstock.com; **29:** (b) © iStock.com/dardespot; **30:** (bl) Fuse/Getty Images; **30:** (br) © maoyunping/Shutterstock.com; **31:** (tr) © wiklander/Shutterstock.com; **33:** (t) © KARNT THASSANAPHAK/Shutterstock.com; **33:** (tm) © iStock.com/RichLegg; **33:** (m) © Steve Design/Shutterstock.com; **33:** (bm) © iStock.com/NikkosDaskalakis; **33:** (b) © Refat/Shutterstock.com; **34:** (t) © photographee/eu/Shutterstock.com; **34:** (b) © TijanaM/Shutterstock.com; **35:** (b) © Hasloo Group Production Studio/Shutterstock.com; **36:** (t) Tim Boyle/Getty Images News/Getty Images; **36:** (m) MICHAEL NICHOLS/National Geographic Creative; **36:** (b) © iStock.com/EdStock; **37:** (mr) © iStock.com/skodonnell; **39:** (t) © Marco Rubino/Shutterstock.com; **39:** (b) © iStock.com/nmaxfield; **40:** (t) © iStock.com/brickrena; **40:** (tm) © iStock.com/beemore; **40:** (mb) © Gillian Mowbray/Shutterstock.com; **40:** (b) © Knumina Studios/Shutterstock.com; **41:** Witthaya/iStock/Getty Images; **42:** (l) David Bank/AWL Images/Getty Images; **42:** (r) LUIS ACOSTA/AFP/Getty Images; **43:** (b) Bettmann/CORBIS; **45:** (t) © iStock.com/sharply_done; **45:** (m) © iStock.com/Solidago; **45:** (b) Darrin Klimek/Digital Vision/Getty Images; **46:** (t) Mike Powell/Digital Vision/Getty Images; **46:** (tm) Hemera Technologies/AbleStock.com/Getty Images; **46:** (bm) © bubamarac/Shutterstock.com; **46:** (b) Sean Gallup/Getty Images News/Getty Images; **47:** (t) © Stephen B. Goodwin/Shutterstock.com; **47:** (tm) © Stephen Coburn/Shutterstock.com; **47:** (bm) © iStock.com/Lisa-Blue; **47:** (b) © Micha Klootwijk/Shutterstock.com; **48:** © iStock.com/fotoVoyager; **49:** (t) Medioimages/Photodisc/Getty Images; **49:** (m) © iStock.com/SimmiSimons; **49:** (b) © V. J. Matthew/Shutterstock.com; **52:** (t) © iStock.com/digitalskillet; **52:** (b) © iStock.com/morrowlight; **53:** (t) © iStock.com/isitsharp; **54:** (tm) © Jim Parkin/Shutterstock.com; **55:** (t) © iStock.com/LUGO; **55:** (tm) © iStock.com/dennysb; **55:** (bm) © Petur Asgeirsson/Shutterstock.com; **55:** (b) Fuse/Getty Images; **57:** (tr) © Olga Sapegina/Shutterstock.com; **58:** (t) © Val Thoermer/Shutterstock.com; **58:** (m) Giuseppe Cacace/Stringer/Getty Images News/Getty Images; **58:** (b) © iStock.com/kali9; **59:** (t) Jupiterimages/Photos.com/Getty Images; **59:** (tm) © iStock.com/Burlingham; **59:** (m) © iStock.com/asiseeit; **59:** (bm) Creatas Images/Creatas/Getty Images; **59:** (b) © Joe White/Shutterstock.com; **60:** (b) © Benjamint/Shutterstock.com; **61:** (t) moodboard/moodboard/Getty Images; **61:** (m) © Alexandra Lande/Shutterstock.com; **61:** (b) ROBIN HYNES/National Geographic Creative; **63:** (t) Alaska Stock Images/National Geographic Creative; **63:** (b) © iStock.com/Hanis; **64:** (tl) Hannele Lahti/National Geographic Creative; **65:** (tr) © iStock.com/drbimages; **66:** (b) William Albert Allard/National Geographic Creative; **67:** (t) © John Kershner/Shutterstock.com; **67:** (b) William Albert Allard/National Geographic Creative; **69:** (tr) Purestock/Getty Images; **70:** (tl) © iStock.com/MorePixels; **70:** (tr) © vita khorzhevska/Shutterstock.com; **70:** (ml) © Odua Images/Shutterstock.com; **70:** (mr) © Digital Media Pro/Shutterstock.com; **70:** (bm) © Elena Elisseeva/Shutterstock.com; **70:** (b) © iStock.com/DanielBendjy; **71:** (b) © iStock.com/YinYang; **72:** (mr) James P. Blair/National Geographic Creative; **75:** (tr) © iStock.com/maxhomand; **75:** (t) Jon Feingersh/Blend Images/Getty Images; **75:** (m) © Cara-Foto/Shutterstock.com; **75:** (b) © iStock.com/jacomstephens; **77:** (t) Sovfoto/Universal Images Group/Getty Images; **78:** (mr) JON T. SCHNEEBERGER/National Geographic Creative.

PEOPLE AND PLACES

UNIT 1

Lesson A GRAMMAR AND VOCABULARY

A Complete the sentences with the correct form of the words in the box.

inhabit employment political herding migration
occur ancient hunting sail fishing

1. Christopher Columbus ____________________ from Europe to America for the first time in 1492.
2. Many people go to other countries for ____________________ because there aren't enough jobs in their home country.
3. In ____________________ times, people traveled by walking.
4. Some people in Central Asia still make a living today by ____________________ cows, sheep, and camels.
5. ____________________ is very important in Japan because people there eat a lot of seafood.
6. The first people who ____________________ North America came from Asia.
7. My grandfather came to this country for ____________________ reasons. He disagreed with the government in his old country, so he had many problems there.
8. Today, some people still enjoy ____________________ as a sport. They like to eat the meat from the animals that they kill.
9. Wars often cause ____________________ of large groups of people who need a safer place to live.
10. The accident ____________________ late at night on Wednesday.

B Complete the sentences. Use the present perfect or present perfect continuous form of the verb in parentheses.

1. I ____________________ never ____________________ house. (move)
2. Joshua ____________________ for a job since June. (look)
3. We ____________________ English for two years. (study)
4. Salma ____________________ Canada twice. (visit)
5. Alex ____________________ in Europe since June. (travel)
6. I ____________________ already ____________________ my homework. (finish)

Lesson B GRAMMAR AND VOCABULARY

A Read what these people say, and circle their reasons for staying where they live. For each person, add one more reason to the list.

1. My name is Maryam, and I live in Dubai. I grew up in a smaller town in another part of this country, and I came here to go to college. After I graduated, I got a job in a bank. I live with my aunt and uncle. My parents are still in my hometown, and I go back to visit them often, but I really prefer living here. There aren't many jobs in my hometown, and besides, the entertainment is so much better in Dubai—movies, restaurants, and shopping.

   employment opportunities **ancestors lived there** **good environment**

   climate **having family members nearby** **other:** ____________________

2. My name is Mi-Ja. My husband and I live in a small village in South Korea, near the city of Kwangju. We're farmers, and we grow rice, cabbage, peppers, and other vegetables. My parents were farmers, and their parents were farmers—we've been living on this land for centuries. My sons live in Kwangju, and they want us to come and live with them, but I hate city life. Here, the air is clean, and it's quiet and peaceful. And all my friends are here. What would I do in the city?

   employment opportunities **ancestors lived there** **good environment**

   climate **having family members nearby** **other:** ____________________

3. My name is Richard. All my life, I lived in New York City, but when I retired five years ago, I moved to Florida. I love it here! It's sunny and beautiful every day of the year—and that means I can play golf every day. Golf is my favorite thing in life. I'm not far from the ocean, and I can go to the beach anytime I want. It's too bad that my children are all so far away, but they can visit me anytime they want to. This is the perfect life for me!

   employment opportunities **ancestors lived there** **good environment**

   climate **having family members nearby** **other:** ____________________

B Write about your reasons for staying where you live—or your reasons for moving to a new place.

____

____

____

____

____

____

Lesson C GRAMMAR AND VOCABULARY

A Label the places on the map with the type of climate there.

a. arid **b.** frigid **c.** rainy **d.** snowy **e.** temperate **f.** tropical

B Write answers using *so* + adjective + *that*.

1. How old is the oldest person you've ever talked to? My grandfather is so old that he remembers the first cars in our city.
2. How rich are some movie stars? ______
3. Is it cheap or expensive to buy a house in your country? ______
4. Are you lazy or hardworking? ______
5. How good is your favorite movie? ______
6. Was this exercise easy or difficult? ______

C Describe the place where you live. In the second sentence, use *so* + adjective + *that.*

1. (the weather) *It's* ______.
   It's so ______ *that* ______.
2. (the people) *They're* ______.
   They're ______.
3. (the houses) ______.
   ______.
4. (the streets) ______.
   ______.
5. (the nightlife) ______.
   ______.

Lesson D READING AND WRITING

Australia, the International Nation

Australia is one of the most multicultural countries in the world. Almost one in every four people in Australia was born in another country: 4.8 million people out of a total population of 21 million. More than 40 percent of Australians have at least one parent who was born in another country.

In a sense, nearly all Australians are immigrants. A little more than 200 years ago, Australia was inhabited by about 350,000 native people of many different cultural groups. Then, in 1770, the explorer James Cook sailed along the coast and brought back information about the "new" land to England. In 1787, the British government started sending criminals and poor people to Australia. Later, free settlers came to Australia to start farms. In 1850, gold was discovered there, and more and more people came from Europe and China hoping to get rich. Most of them never returned home, so the population began to grow.

Australia has a huge amount of land, and in the 1940s the government decided that the best way to develop the country was to invite more settlers to come from Europe. To attract immigrants, they offered money and other forms of help. More than 1 million people from Britain moved to Australia then, along with several hundred thousand Europeans who had lost their homes in World War II.

Migration is still growing. In 2012, more than 50,000 people went to Australia to stay permanently. Four main types of people settle there. Some go there because employment and business opportunities are better than in their home country. Others are the children, parents, or other relatives of immigrants who have become Australian citizens. A third group is refugees who are escaping from war or political problems in their home countries. Finally, there are also a few Australians who migrated to another country and now want to come home.

At the same time, Australia also sends immigrants to other countries—a smaller number. Each year, about 60,000 Australians go to live permanently in other countries. With people from so many cultures migrating in and out, Australia is truly a diverse nation.

A Choose the correct answer.

1. The main idea of this article is that ____.
   - **a.** migration is very important in Australia
   - **b.** Australia still needs more people
   - **c.** the first immigrants to Australia came from Britain

2. The article talks about ____.
   - **a.** people who migrate to Australia
   - **b.** people who migrate from Australia
   - **c.** both **a** and **b**

3. Which reason for migration is NOT in the article?
   - **a.** being together with family members
   - **b.** environmental problems
   - **c.** employment

4. Today, the number of people who are moving to Australia is ____.
   - **a.** getting larger
   - **b.** staying the same
   - **c.** getting smaller

5. According to the article, ____ Australians originally came from another country.
   - **a.** 40 percent of
   - **b.** 167,000
   - **c.** 4.8 million

6. The first people from outside migrated to Australia in ____.
   - **a.** 1770
   - **b.** 1787
   - **c.** 1850

B Answer the questions.

1. Which fact in the article surprised you the most?

   ____

   ____

2. Why were you surprised?

   ____

   ____

3. Why are immigrants good for a country?

   ____

   ____

4. Can immigration be bad for a country?

   ____

   ____

C Why do people move to your country? Why do people leave your country? Write about the reasons.

____

____

____

____

UNIT 1

Review

A Solve the crossword puzzle with grammar and vocabulary from this unit.

Across

3. very, very old
5. travel in a boat
6. a climate that is warm and wet
9. live in a place
10. a very cold climate
12. I _______ (study) English for five years. (3 words)
14. The climate here is _______. It rains only a few times a year.
15. a climate with a lot of rain
16. _______ places are good for skiing.
17. happen
18. killing animals for food

Down

1. related to the government
2. a climate that isn't very hot or very cold
4. catching fish and sea animals
7. I _______ (eat) lunch, so I'm not hungry now. (2 words)
8. caring for a group of animals
11. movement from one place to another
13. work done to earn a living

B Circle the correct words to complete the paragraph.

My cousin (1) (has been moving | has moved) to Australia. He says there are better (2) (climate | employment) opportunities there and the (3) (environment | political) is cleaner. Australia is (4) (that | so) big (5) (that | so) there are a lot of places with small populations. My cousin (6) (has been traveling | was traveling) a lot since he arrived. He tries to visit somewhere new when he has free time. He is very happy in his new home. He says migration (7) (has been making | has made) Australia a great place to live because you meet people from lots of different countries.

THE MIND

UNIT 2

Lesson A GRAMMAR AND VOCABULARY

memorize	react	cell	retain
landmark	visualize	portion	
recalling	mental	technique	

A Complete the sentences with the correct form of the words in the box.

1. The Eiffel Tower is a ____________ in Paris.
2. ____________ information is important when you are taking an exam.
3. One ____________ of your brain is used for language and words.
4. When I feel stressed, I like to ____________ sitting on a beautiful beach.
5. London taxi drivers have special ____________ abilities to make maps in their minds.
6. Firefighters and police officers must ____________ quickly in dangerous situations.
7. Your brain is made up of millions of special ____________.
8. In history class last year, we ____________ all the names of the presidents of our country.
9. To ____________ new information in your brain, you must use it so that you don't forget it.
10. My ____________ for remembering English words is to write them ten times.

B Complete the sentences with your own ideas. Use gerunds.

1. I remember important dates by ____.
2. ____ is a good way to meet new people.
3. I sometimes worry about ____.
4. I'm looking forward to ____ next weekend.
5. ____ is important for my country's future.
6. ____ is the best way to learn vocabulary.

C Mr. Carter is a foreign businessman in your city. Complete the conversation with your own ideas. Use gerunds.

Mr. Carter: I'm new in your city. What's the best way to learn all the streets and places here?

You: ____

____

Mr. Carter: I studied your language for a year, but I can't speak it very well. What's the best way to improve my speaking?

You: ____

____

Mr. Carter: I really want to learn more about the culture of your country. What are some good ways for foreigners to do that?

You: ____

____

Lesson B GRAMMAR AND VOCABULARY

A Complete the chart about your senses. Use your dictionary as needed.

Sense	Verb	Body part
sight		
	smell	
touch		skin
	hear	
	taste	

B Imagine you are the person in the pictures. What do you notice? Write one sentence for each of your senses. Use your imagination!

1. a. (sight) *I see monkeys playing in a big tree.*
   b. (hearing) ______
   c. (touch) ______
   d. (smell) ______
   e. (taste) ______
2. a. (sight) ______
   b. (hearing) ______
   c. (touch) ______
   d. (smell) ______
   e. (taste) ______

Lesson C GRAMMAR AND VOCABULARY

A Circle the correct word to complete each sentence.

1. Dr. Kim works in a (laboratory | research) in the medical building at the university.
2. Jason is doing (theory | research) on how people can get over their fears.
3. Scientists have a new (theory | survey) that people learn to be afraid of snakes.
4. The class did a (survey | experiment) and asked 100 people a lot of questions.
5. In the (conclusion | experiment), the scientists gave two groups of dogs different food to eat.
6. Professor Sanchez talked about the (conduct | results) of her research.
7. Scientists (research | conduct) experiments to test their theories.
8. The (conclusion | laboratory) was that people's biggest fear is accidents.

B Dave is afraid of a lot of things. Match the words to a reason, and then write sentences with *may*, *might*, or *could*.

1. dogs	a. get lost
2. foreign food	b. get a stomachache
3. visiting big cities	c. run into a shark
4. boats	d. fall in the water
5. swimming	e. have a terrible accident
6. driving	f. bite him

1. *He's afraid of dogs because they could bite him.*
2. ______________________
3. ______________________
4. ______________________
5. ______________________
6. ______________________

C What are three things that make you afraid? Explain using *may*, *might*, or *could*.

1. I don't like ______________ because ______________ ______________________.
2. I'm afraid of ______________ because ______________ ______________________.
3. ______________ make(s) me nervous because ______________ ______________________.

Lesson D READING AND WRITING

The Mind-Body Connection

Norman Cousins was a famous American magazine editor. In 1964, he returned from an overseas trip and became very ill. In the hospital, he had terrible pain and couldn't move his body. Doctors told him he had a serious disease called *ankylosing spondylitis* and said he had only 1 chance in 500 of surviving. They gave him powerful drugs, but his condition only got worse.

Cousins had read about a theory that negative emotions can harm your health. He believed that positive emotions were good for your health, and he decided to try an experiment. He would fill his days with good feelings and laughter and see if that might improve his condition.

He left the hospital and moved into a hotel room. There, he got a large supply of funny TV programs and copies of old Marx Brothers movies and cartoons. He also hired a nurse to read funny stories to him. His plan was to spend the whole day laughing and thinking about happy things. On his first night in the hotel, Cousins found that laughing at the movies helped his body produce chemicals that reduced pain. For the first time in weeks, he could sleep comfortably for a few hours. Every time the pain came back, he watched another funny movie and laughed until he felt better.

Over time, Cousins was able to measure changes in his body with blood tests. He found that the harmful chemicals in his body decreased at least 5 percent every time he watched a funny movie. After a short time, he was able to stop taking all of his medications. Finally his condition improved so much that he could go back to work.

Cousins later wrote a book about how laughter and happiness helped him to survive a deadly illness. Many people didn't believe his story and said that his doctors were wrong about his disease. But since then, research has found that emotions do have a strong effect on physical health, and experiments found that laughter can help to reduce pain. Scientists today are working to understand the ways that our minds affect our bodies.

A Circle **T** for *true*, **F** for *false*, or **NI** for *no information* (if the answer is not in the reading).

1.	Norman Cousins became ill while he was traveling in another country.	T	F	NI
2.	Doctors told Cousins that he would probably die from his disease.	T	F	NI
3.	Drugs helped to stop the pain of Cousins's disease.	T	F	NI
4.	Cousins started watching movies because he was bored.	T	F	NI
5.	Cousins spent a lot of time laughing every day.	T	F	NI
6.	Movies were better than funny stories for stopping pain.	T	F	NI
7.	When Cousins wrote his book, everyone agreed with him.	T	F	NI
8.	Scientists have done research on using laughter to stop pain.	T	F	NI

B Number the events in order.

____ Cousins watched funny movies and cartoons all day.

____ Cousins went back to work.

____ Cousins went to a hospital.

____ Doctors told Cousins he had a terrible disease.

____ Researchers found that Cousins's ideas were right.

____ Cousins took many medications.

____ The pain didn't get better.

____ People didn't agree with Cousins's ideas.

____ Cousins felt much better.

▲ Norman Cousins

C Can your mind make your body sick or well? Write about your opinion, and give reasons and examples.

UNIT 2

Review

A Solve the crossword puzzle using grammar and vocabulary from this unit.

Across

1. to learn exactly
3. I'm thinking about (become) _______ a teacher.
7. a place where scientists work
9. the smallest part of your body
11. do an experiment
13. I'm tired of (sit) _______ in an office all day.
15. a test that scientists do to see if something is true
16. a scientific idea
17. the sense you use your nose for

Down

1. If I drive there, I _______ get lost.
2. remembering
4. I don't like (fly) _______ because airplanes make me nervous.
5. the sense you use your eyes for
6. something you decide after looking at all the information
8. I'm afraid of that dog because he _______ bite me.
10. make a picture in your mind
12. If I speak English, I _______ make a mistake.
14. related to your mind

B Circle the correct words to complete the paragraph.

When you are learning a language, using different learning strategies can help you. For example, (1) (visualize | visualizing) an image for a new word (2) (may | conduct) help. But for some people, (3) (hearing | hear) the new word a lot helps them; they learn better using their sense of (4) (sight | sound). Different people use different (5) (techniques | experiments) to help them (6) (research | memorize) new words.

CHANGING PLANET

UNIT 3

Lesson A GRAMMAR AND VOCABULARY

A Complete the article with the correct form of the words from the box.

oil	global warming
increase	deforestation
sea level	led to
extreme	climate change
conservation	drought

Save the Planet!

- Save the forests by using wood and paper carefully. ______________ is a serious problem when too many trees are cut down.
- Turn lights off when you aren't using them, and turn your computer off at night. ______________ of electricity is important for the future.
- Drive less. An ______________ in the use of buses, trains, and other public transportation will help save ______________.
- Think about how you affect the environment. Burning coal in electric power plants has ______________ the earth's temperature getting hotter. This ______________ is melting the polar ice, and the ______________ in some places is getting higher. But warming isn't the only kind of ______________. Many places are having more ______________ weather, such as hurricanes, ______________, and very cold winters.

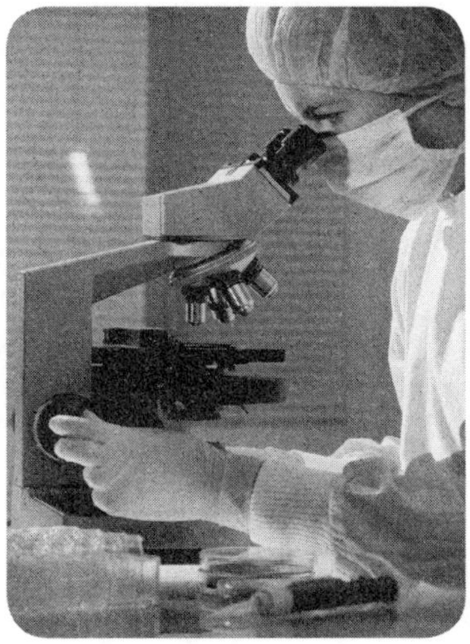

B Write the tense and then rewrite the sentence in the passive voice using the same tense.

1. A famous professor wrote that book. Tense: simple past tense
   That book was written by a famous professor.
2. Bees make honey. Tense: ______________
   ____
3. Our teacher will check our homework. Tense: ______________
   ____
4. The police have found the lost children. Tense: ______________
   ____
5. The government is building many new schools. Tense: ______________
   ____
6. My mother always bakes my birthday cake. Tense: ______________
   ____
7. The scientists didn't conduct the experiment. Tense: ______________
   ____

Lesson B GRAMMAR AND VOCABULARY

A Label the types of weather.

flood extreme heat drought extreme cold hurricane

1. ______________

2. ______________

3. ______________

4. ______________

5. ______________

B What could be done in your school to help the environment? Complete the chart with your ideas. Use *could be.*

teaching people about the environment	1. Posters could be made. 2.
electricity and energy	1. 2.
garbage	1. 2.
using less paper	1. 2.

C Underline the sounds that link together. Then read the sentences out loud.

1. I gave him my e-mail address so he could write to me.
2. Jim and I live very close to this school.
3. I think hurricanes are the worst type of extreme weather.
4. We try to learn at least ten new words every day.
5. Do you think Cassie will invite me to her party?
6. I went to class on Monday.

Lesson C GRAMMAR AND VOCABULARY

A Write each number in words.

1. 2,047 ____________________
2. 50,000,000 ____________________
3. 78,000 ____________________
4. 731,000 ____________________
5. 115,200 ____________________
6. 4,650,001 ____________________

B Answer the questions. Write the numbers in words.

1. How many people live in your city? about ____________________
2. What's the population of your country? ____________________
3. How many English words do you know? ____________________
4. How much does a car cost in your country? ____________________
5. How much does a house cost in your city? ____________________

C Complete the sentences with the simple past or past perfect tense.

1. Mami had never spoken (speak, never) English before she went (go) to New York last summer.
2. I was late for class, and the teacher __________ (collect, already) the homework when I __________ (come) in.
3. The children __________ (be, not) hungry for dinner because they __________ (eat) a lot of candy after school.
4. Danny __________ (hate, always) jazz until he __________ (go) to a concert last year.
5. By the time the baseball game __________ (start), the rain __________ (stop), so everyone __________ (be) happy.

D Write sentences about yourself using the past perfect tense.

1. By the time I was ten years old, ____________________
____
2. By the time I went to bed last night, ____________________
____
3. (your own idea) ____________________
____________________.

Lesson D READING AND WRITING

What Can One City Do?

People around the world are concerned about global warming and are talking about ways to stop it. The city of Cambridge, Massachusetts, in the United States, is doing more than just talking. Cambridge wants to become a world leader in energy-efficient buildings.

Today, Naema Omar is improving her 80-year-old house in Cambridge. To keep the heat inside in the winter, she is filling the space inside the walls with insulation. Insulation is usually made from chemicals, but in her house, she is using something new—insulation made from recycled blue jeans and other clothes. She has also put in a new type of light called an LED lamp that uses only a tiny amount of electricity. The lightbulbs in it last for 20 to 30 years before needing to be changed.

But eco-friendly insulation and lighting are much more expensive than the usual kind, and many people in Cambridge can't afford them. A group called Cambridge Energy Alliance (CEA) is working to solve this problem. They want to help every resident and business in the city conserve energy. People can ask the group to come and look at their house or office building. The CEA then makes them a plan to save 15 to 30 percent on heating, gas, water, and electricity. Then the group helps people borrow money to pay for the improvements. The money that people save by being more efficient should be enough to pay back the loan.

Ten years ago, the city of Cambridge decided to try to reduce its carbon emissions. More than 80 percent of the carbon dioxide produced in Cambridge comes from buildings—not from cars. If the program is successful, it will not only save a lot of energy but also make new jobs for local people. Workers will be needed to put in insulation, install better doors and windows, and make other energy improvements on buildings. The CEA hopes that their program will be an example for other cities.

A Choose the correct answer.

1. Naema Omar is trying to save energy for ____.
   a. heat b. lighting c. both **a** and **b**
2. One problem with saving energy is that ____.
   a. it isn't always successful b. you need money c. you can't do it in old houses
3. The Cambridge Energy Alliance is working to save energy in ____.
   a. buildings b. cars c. both **a** and **b**
4. If people need money to do home energy projects, ____ helps them get it.
   a. their bank b. the CEA c. the government
5. The city of Cambridge wants to ____.
   a. stop producing carbon dioxide b. help other cities save energy c. make efficient new houses
6. Saving energy can ____.
   a. save money for people b. make new jobs c. both **a** and **b**

B Number these steps in order.

____ The Cambridge Energy Alliance makes a plan for the home.
__1__ People want to save energy in their homes.
____ People contact the Cambridge Energy Alliance.
____ People use the money to make energy improvements in their homes.
____ The Cambridge Energy Alliance goes to the home.
____ People pay back the loan with the money they save on energy.
____ The Cambridge Energy Alliance helps people get money.

C Write about three things that people in your country can do to save energy. Why should they do these things?

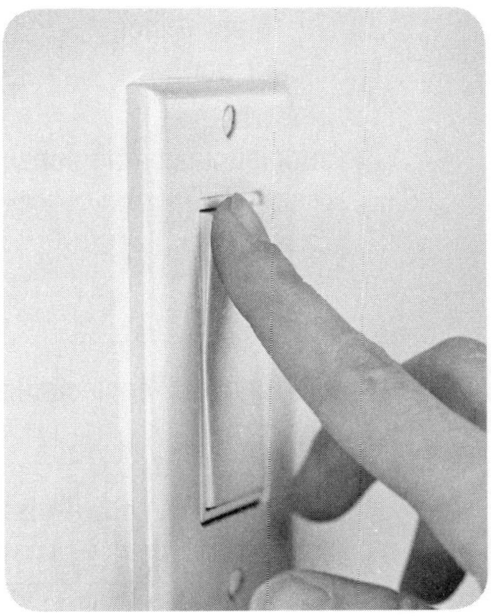

____
____
____
____
____
____
____
____

UNIT 3

Review

A Solve the crossword puzzle with grammar and vocabulary from this unit.

Across

4. 1,000,000 (2 words)
6. a black liquid burned for fuel
12. how high the water in the ocean is (2 words)
13. 200 (2 words)
14. get larger
15. 600,000 (3 words)
16. That movie was made _______ two students.

Down

1. The bank _______ (rob) last night. (2 words)
2. 2,000,020 (3 words)
3. cutting down trees over a large area
5. Earth is getting hotter because of _______. (2 words)
7. Many things _______ (can, do) to save energy. (3 words)
8. 10,000 (2 words)
9. By four o'clock, I _______ (finish) all my work. (2 words)
10. saving or protecting the environment
11. A lot of pollution _______ (cause) by cars. (2 words)

B Complete the paragraph with words from the box. Put the verbs in the correct form.

conservation	hurricanes	study	affect	extreme	global warming	start

Before I (1) ____________________ to work as a conservationist last year, I (2) ____________________ environmental engineering at university. (3) ____________________ is very important to me. We all know that our planet (4) ____________________ by population growth and (5) ____________________, but we need to find solutions to the problems they have caused. More and more people (6) ____________________ by (7) ____________________ weather every year. Floods and (8) ____________________ have destroyed homes all over the world.

MONEY VS. WEALTH

UNIT 4

Lesson A GRAMMAR AND VOCABULARY

A Circle the correct answer to show the meaning of the vocabulary word in **bold.**

1. If your **expenses** are high, you (get | spend) a lot of money.
2. Your **income** is all the money that you (pay | receive).
3. Those jeans are a real **bargain.** They're so (expensive | cheap)!
4. I **lend** money to people in my family if they have (a problem | a birthday).
5. You really need a **budget.** You need (a plan | a wallet) for all your money.
6. I **borrowed** some money from my friend because (she | I) didn't have any money.
7. If you pay for something with **cash,** you use (coins and bills | a credit card).
8. Risa has **debt.** Every month she (pays money to the bank | gets a big salary).

B Answer the questions.

1. Do you ever borrow money? Why or why not? ____________________

   ____
2. Do you lend money? Why or why not? ____________________

   ____
3. What are your biggest expenses every month? ____________________

   ____
4. What was the best bargain you ever found? ____________________

   ____

C Tomoko is a university student in Tokyo. Complete the paragraph with the correct form of the verbs—gerund or infinitive.

"I hope __________ (go) to Europe next year, so I'm trying __________ (save) enough money. Now I avoid __________ (eat) in restaurants, because that's very expensive. And I've given up __________ (go) to movies. So far, I've saved 100,000 yen—that's about $1,000—but it's not enough. I want __________ (stay) in Europe for at least one month, so I need a lot more money. I've decided __________ (live) with my parents, because my apartment is very expensive. And I've considered (get) __________ a part-time job. But my expenses are so high. I have to pay for my books, my cell phone, and my food. And wearing nice clothes is very important to me!"

D What should Tomoko do? Write ideas using a gerund or infinitive.

1. try *She should* ____________________
2. stop ____________________
3. begin ____________________

Lesson B GRAMMAR AND VOCABULARY

A Read the article and answer the questions with information from the article and your own ideas.

The Value of Gold

There are three reasons why gold is so valuable. First, it is beautiful. People in almost every culture have used it in jewelry and works of art. Second, it is useful. It carries electricity well, and many electronic devices like computers and cell phones contain small amounts of gold. Finally, it is scarce. It is found in only a few places in the world, and often thousands of kilograms of rocks must be processed to find just a few grams of gold. For these reasons, the price of gold is always high.

1. Why is gold valuable? ____________, ____________, ____________
2. Do people in your country think gold is valuable? ____________
3. In your opinion, is gold the most valuable thing in the world? Explain your answer. ____________

____

B Think about the three most valuable things you have (for example, *a picture of my grandmother*). Then check (✓) the reasons why each thing is valuable to you.

	Item #1: ______	Item #2: ______	Item #3: ______
a. It cost a lot of money.			
b. It's important in my life.			
c. It's very useful.			
d. It came from someone I love.			
e. It's very old.			
f. It's unusual.			
g. Many people want to have this.			
h. other reason (write the reason) ____________			

C Write about one of the items in exercise **B** in your notebook. Describe it and explain why it's valuable to you.

Lesson C GRAMMAR AND VOCABULARY

A Match the banking terms with their meanings.

1. savings account ___
2. teller ___
3. PIN number ___
4. deposit ___
5. receipt ___
6. ATM ___
7. checking account ___
8. withdraw ___

a. a paper that tells how much money you got or spent
b. a bank account where you keep money to spend later
c. put money into the bank
d. take money out of the bank
e. a person who works in a bank
f. a bank account that you can use to pay for things
g. a secret number that you use with a bank machine
h. a bank machine

B Fill in the correct form of the verb, active or passive. Use the correct tense.

1. Today, ATMs ______________ (find) in countries around the world.
2. The money ______________ (steal) yesterday by two men. The police ______________ (find) them later.
3. That TV program ______________ (watch) by millions of people last night.
4. In the past, credit cards ______________ (use) only by adults. Now teenagers ______________ (get) them, too.
5. My birthday dinner ______________ (cook) by my mother. My sister ______________ (make) my cake.

C Make each sentence passive. Form the correct tense with *be*.

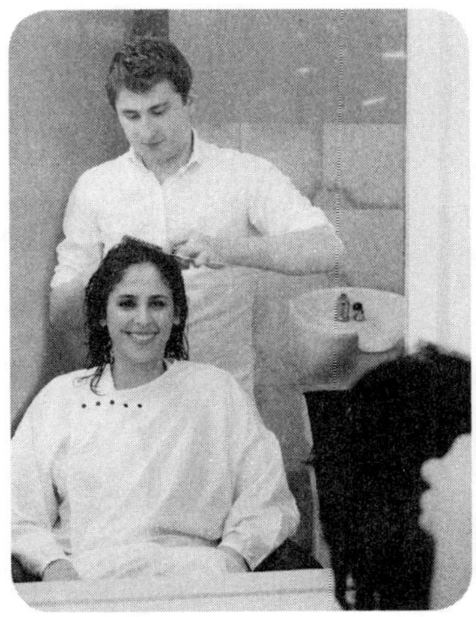

1. George cuts her hair. ______________________________
2. George cut her hair yesterday. ______________________________
3. George is going to cut her hair. ______________________________
4. George will cut her hair. ______________________________
5. George might cut her hair. ______________________________

D Circle the agent. If the agent is not needed, rewrite the sentence without it.

1. The first coins were made by people in Turkey 3,000 years ago.

   ____

2. Many flowers for perfume are grown in France by farmers.

   ____

3. The Mona Lisa was painted by Leonardo da Vinci.

   ____

4. Some very good cars are produced by workers in Korea.

   ____

Lesson D READING AND WRITING

Banknotes: Facts About Paper Money

The first kinds of money used in different countries were gold, silver, and other valuable things. But before long, new kinds of money were needed. There wasn't enough metal to make coins, and people had trouble buying things. In addition, coins were difficult to carry around—especially for rich people in China. The coins there had a hole in the middle, and people put a string through the coins. These long strings of coins were extremely heavy.

In about 600 AD, Chinese merchants found a solution to these problems. The merchants would leave their strings of coins with a government official and get a piece of paper that said how many strings of coins they had left there. They could use this paper to buy things from a seller, and the seller could take the paper to get the coins. These papers were the first banknotes, or paper money.

By about 960 AD, the government of China was printing pictures on paper to make official banknotes. The first paper money was used in Europe in 1574, when banks in Holland made very small paper "coins." Sweden printed the first banknotes in Europe in 1660.

Today, countries around the world have their own banknotes. Large countries print their own banknotes, and a company in England called De La Rue prints banknotes for many smaller countries like Honduras, Sri Lanka, and Fiji. Most banknotes are still printed on very heavy paper, but some countries, like Australia, use very thin plastic. Because it's easy to make false banknotes, countries put many special features in their banknotes. They use ink that changes color, metal threads in the paper, and even plastic windows in the money. These make the banknotes difficult to copy.

But there is still one big problem with banknotes that hasn't been solved. Metal coins last for a long time, but banknotes quickly become dirty and wear out. An average banknote lasts only a few years. In the United States, old banknotes are collected by the government, cut in small pieces, and recycled into other paper products. In Australia, the plastic banknotes are melted and made into garbage cans!

A Circle **T** for *true*, **F** for *false*, or **NI** for *no information* (if the answer isn't in the reading).

1.	Coins were made before banknotes.	T	F	NI
2.	Banknotes don't last as long as metal coins.	T	F	NI
3.	Some people don't like to use banknotes.	T	F	NI
4.	*Banknote* is another name for paper money.	T	F	NI
5.	Old banknotes can be recycled and made into new things.	T	F	NI
6.	Sweden made the first banknotes in the world.	T	F	NI
7.	People don't make as many false banknotes now because they are difficult to copy.	T	F	NI
8.	Banknotes were invented in 1574.	T	F	NI

B Answer the questions.

Which country/countries in the article . . .

1. had the first banknotes in Europe? ______________________
2. has a company that prints banknotes for other countries? ____________
3. makes garbage cans from old money? ____________________
4. had the first paper money? ________________________
5. made coins from paper? __________________________
6. don't print their own money? _______________________
7. makes old money into paper products? __________________

C What picture is on the smallest banknote in your country? Why was that picture used? Imagine your country wants to make a new banknote. What picture should be on it? Explain your reasons.

____

____

____

____

____

____

____

____

____

Review

A Solve the crossword puzzle with grammar and vocabulary from this unit.

Across

5. a bank account where you keep money to spend later (2 words)
9. money that you have to spend
10. give money to someone who will pay you back later
12. a plan for spending money
13. a bank machine
15. a person who works in a bank
16. take money out of the bank

Down

1. secret number for an ATM (2 words)
2. something cheap or on sale
3. get money that you will give back later
4. money that you receive for working
6. Credit cards ___ (use) around the world today. (2 words)
7. The first coins ___ (make) in Turkey. (2 words)
8. money owed to a bank or a company
11. put money in the bank
14. coins and paper money

B Circle the correct words to complete the paragraph.

My (1) (bargain | expenses) are really high at the moment because I stopped (2) (to live | living) with my parents. Now I have to pay rent for my apartment, buy food, and pay for everything myself. I have to make a (3) (budget | income) every month so I can pay for everything. I decided (4) (to open | opening) a (5) (PIN number | savings account) at the bank to help me organize my finances. Last month, I (6) (borrowed | was borrowed) some money to buy a car. The money (7) (lent | was lent) to me by the bank. That money has helped me, but now I have (8) (bargain | debt)!

SURVIVAL

UNIT 5

Lesson A GRAMMAR AND VOCABULARY

A Match the words with their meanings.

1. emergency ____
2. panic ____
3. natural disaster ____
4. preparation ____
5. supplies ____
6. equipment ____
7. evacuate ____
8. first aid ____
9. cope with ____
10. situation ____

a. all the things that are happening at one time
b. food, clothes, and other things needed for daily life
c. an accident caused by nature, like an earthquake
d. leave your house because of danger
e. tools that you need to do something
f. a dangerous time
g. simple medical treatment
h. getting ready before doing something
i. succeed in dealing with a problem
j. become very afraid

B Write sentences about these unreal conditions and results.

1. condition: I/see an accident __ result: I/call for help
   If I saw an accident, I would call for help.
2. condition: we/know first aid __ result: we/help a lot of people
   ____
3. result: I/visit my grandparents more often __ condition: I/have more time
   ____
4. condition: he/not know how to swim __ result: he/be afraid of water
   ____
5. result: I/not give any homework __ condition: I/be the teacher of this class
   ____

C Look at the pictures of unreal situations on the right. Write sentences about what you would do in each one.

1. ______________________________
2. ______________________________
3. ______________________________
4. ______________________________

Lesson B GRAMMAR AND VOCABULARY

Read the survival situations. Write the possible results of each plan. Then choose the best plan and write your reasons.

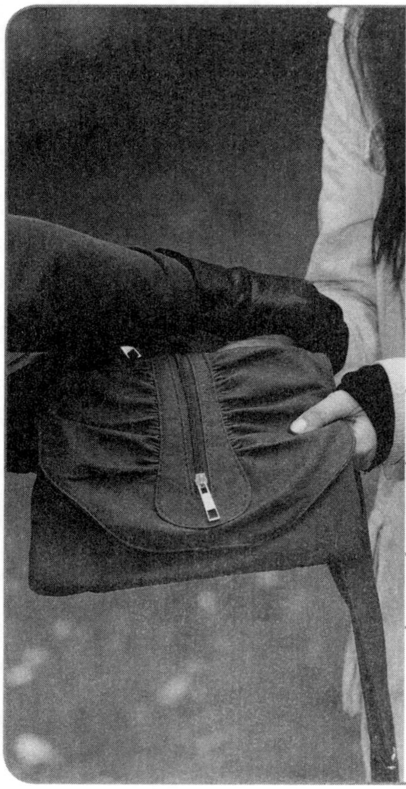

Situation 1: You are walking down a dark street at night in your city. A man steps up to you and says, "Give me all your money!" His hands are in his pockets. You can't see if he is holding anything. You have about $20 in your wallet.

Plan	Possible results
1. Run away.	The man might catch me, and then I would have a bigger problem.
2. Give the man your money.	
3. Shout, "Help me! Help me!"	
4. Say, "I don't have any money."	
5. (your own idea)	

The best plan is number _____. Reasons:

Situation 2: You are on vacation in the mountains, 50 miles from the nearest town. Your car goes off the road. The weather is very cold but sunny. You are not hurt, but your car can't be driven. Very few people travel on this road. You have food and water for two days.

Plan	Possible results
1. Stay inside your car and wait for people to find you.	
2. Take the food and water with you. Start walking to the town.	
3. Build a big fire outside the car so that people can find you.	
4. Eat the food and drink the water. Then walk to a bigger road.	
5. (your own idea)	

The best plan is number _____. Reasons:

Lesson C GRAMMAR AND VOCABULARY

A Match the words with their meanings.

1. species ____
2. ban ____
3. reserve ____
4. preservation ____
5. ecosystem ____
6. predatory ____
7. restore ____
8. endangered ____

a. bring back into good condition
b. all the plants and animals that live in a particular place
c. a place where hunting and fishing are not allowed
d. close to extinction
e. hunting and killing other animals for food
f. a scientific word for a kind of plant or animal
g. keeping something in good condition
h. to not allow something

B Write sentences using *wish*.

1. Rachel doesn't like her job. She wishes she had a different job.
2. My city doesn't have any parks. ________
3. Josh lives far from his school. ________
4. I don't have a lot of friends. ________
5. I'm not lying on the beach now. ________
6. Katie spends a lot of money. ________
7. I have to wash the dishes every day. ________

C Rafael is unhappy about his life. Write sentences about his wishes.

1. He wishes ________
____
2. ________
____
3. ________
____
4. (your own idea) ________
____

D Write your own wishes about these things.

1. (Your city) I wish ________
2. (Your country) ________
3. (The world) ________

Lesson D READING AND WRITING

Ready for Anything

Every day, newspapers are filled with articles about natural disasters like floods, earthquakes, and hurricanes. These emergencies can occur in every country in the world, so it's important to be ready for them. There are three important things you should do at home to prepare.

First, stock up on emergency supplies. You should keep enough food and water for at least three days in your house. Choose food that can be stored for a long time and food that can be eaten without cooking. Canned foods such as soup, fish, meat, and fruit are good choices. You can also store dry foods like crackers and cookies. Be sure to store food that you like and include a few special treats like candy or nuts. In an emergency situation, it's nice to have something to cheer you up. If you have babies, small children, or elderly people in your family, remember to include any special foods that they need. And be sure to keep plenty of water. Each person needs 1 gallon (4 liters) of water per day for drinking and basic washing.

In addition, think about equipment you might need for the kinds of disasters that happen in your country. You might need blankets, very warm clothes, flashlights, or plastic bags. Think about possible situations, and buy the things that would be needed.

Finally, plan what you will do in case you need to evacuate your home. Decide where you will go. It's good to arrange a meeting place in advance—such as a relative's home or a big public building. Also, plan a way to contact other family members if you become separated. Be sure that all family members know the phone number of a contact person in another city.

People don't like to think about natural disasters, but a little bit of preparation can save lives. Following these steps will help you be ready for any kind of emergency.

A Complete the outline with information from the reading.

Ready for Anything

I. Natural disasters happen every day.

Examples: ____________, ____________, ____________

People should prepare at home for disasters.

II. Three steps to prepare for disasters

A. ______________________________

1. canned foods

examples: __________, __________, __________, __________

2. __________

examples: crackers, cookies

3. treats

examples: __________, __________

4. water

__________ for each person for each day

B. ______________________________

examples: blankets, very warm clothes, flashlights, or plastic bags

C. ______________________________

a. decide ______________________________

b. plan ______________________________

III. Conclusion

A. People don't ______________________________

B. Preparing ______________________________

B What is the most common emergency situation in your country? Write about what you would do if it happened to you.

____

____

____

____

____

____

UNIT 5

Review

A Solve the crossword puzzle with grammar and vocabulary from this unit.

Across

5. simple medical help (2 words)
7. a time when your life is in danger
10. If I had time, I _______ (go) to visit my sister in London. (2 words)
12. become very afraid
13. tools you need to do something
14. put something back into good condition
17. what you do to keep something in good condition
18. leave your house because of danger

Down

1. one kind of plant or animal
2. Floods are a common natural _______ in my country.
3. things you need for everyday life
4. what you do to get ready for something
6. Jack wishes he _______ (not have) to get up early. (2 words)
8. I wish I _______ (can speak) Chinese. (2 words)
9. I wish I _______ (be) rich!
11. all the plants and animals in a place
15. not allowed
16. If you _______ with a bad situation, you get through it successfully.

B Circle the correct words to complete the paragraph.

If you (1) (would be | were) in an earthquake or a hurricane or some other (2) (ecosystem | natural disaster), you (3) (wouldn't be able to | weren't able to) do anything to prevent it. That's why (4) (preservation | preparation) is so important. Nobody wishes they (5) (are | were) in an emergency (6) (equipment | situation), but if you are prepared, it is easier to (7) (evacuate | cope) with it. It is recommended that you have a (8) (first aid | panic) kit and other (9) (reserves | supplies) like food, water, blankets, and a flashlight. It is also very important not to (10) (cope | panic).

Lesson A GRAMMAR AND VOCABULARY

techniques	style	sculptures	paintings	depict
represent	realistic	aware	diverse	abstract

A Complete the sentences with the correct form of the words in the box.

1. ____________________ art does not show things as they really are. It is not ____________________.
2. Some people prefer art that ____________________ real life.
3. Public art often includes ____________________. They can be made of different materials: stone, wood, metal, or plastic, for example.
4. Large ____________________ on walls are called murals.
5. The knotted gun sculpture outside the United Nations building in New York ____________________ peace.
6. Artists may use the same ____________________ when they paint, but every artist has his or her own unique ____________________.
7. The beauty of art is that it is so ____________________; there are so many different kinds.
8. Sometimes artists aren't ____________________ of how their work influences people.

B Write what each person said. Use reported speech and make all the necessary changes.

1. Tomoko: "I have a headache." *Tomoko said she had a headache.*
2. Rita: "I live in New York." ____________________
3. The president: "I have a plan to help our country." ____________________
4. Mohammed: "I can't go to the movie because I'm doing my homework." ____________________
5. Cathy: "I haven't been to the new museum." ____________________
6. Chris and Dennis: "We really like living here." ____________________
7. Emily: "I'm going to my hometown tomorrow." ____________________

C Think of a very important phone call that you had. What did the other person say? Write sentences in reported speech.

1. ____________________
2. ____________________

Lesson B GRAMMAR AND VOCABULARY

A Look at each painting and write down your ideas.

Painting 1

1. Describe the painting. ____________________
____
2. Think of a title for this painting. "____________________"
3. Where is a good place to put this painting? Why? ____________________
____

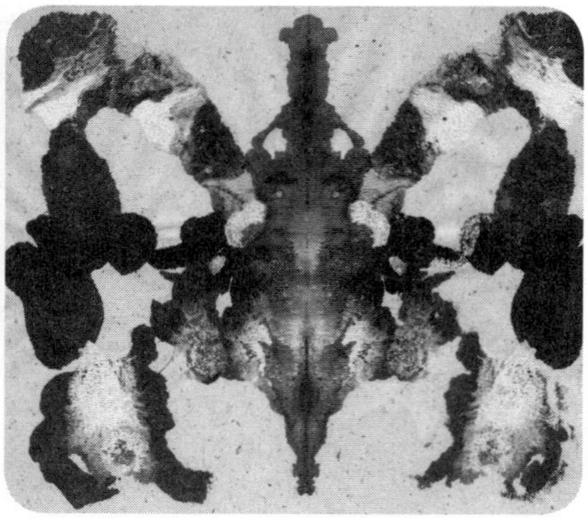

Painting 2

1. Describe the painting. ____________________
____
2. Think of a title for this painting. "____________________"
3. Where is a good place to put this painting? Why? ____________________
____

Painting 3

1. Describe the painting. ____________________
____
2. Think of a title for this painting. "____________________"
3. Where is a good place to put this painting? Why? ____________________
____

Painting 4

1. Describe the painting. ____________________
____
2. Think of a title for this painting. "____________________"
3. Where is a good place to put this painting? Why? ____________________
____

B Answer the questions.

1. Which painting do you like the most? Why? ____________________
____
2. Which painting do you like the least? Why? ____________________
____

Lesson C GRAMMAR AND VOCABULARY

A Complete the chart with items from the box. Then add one more idea to each box.

glass	leather	textiles	stone
vase			
wood	**bronze**	**silver**	**clay**

bronze statue	glass vase
wooden box	leather bag
decorative plate	stone sculpture
handwoven cloth	piece of jewelry

B Combine the two sentences by using an adjective clause. Use *who* or *that*.

1. Sandy has a friend. The friend makes metal sculptures.
   Sandy has a friend who makes metal sculptures.
2. I want to get a cheap camera. The camera takes good pictures.
   ______
3. The dictionary is on the table. The dictionary is mine.
   ______
4. I read a great book. The book was written by a 16-year-old girl.
   ______
5. I know a doctor. The doctor works with elderly people.
   ______
6. Sanjay likes paintings. The paintings have a lot of bright colors.
   ______

C Write sentences with adjective clauses about the kinds of things you like/dislike/enjoy/hate/love.

1. music I like music that ______
2. movies ______
3. art ______
4. food ______

Biographies of Great Artists: Frida Kahlo

"Casa Azul" where Frida Kahlo lived

The two Fridas, 1939

Frida Kahlo was born in Mexico in 1907. As a small child, she was very happy and ran and laughed all the time—even in church. When she was six years old, her life changed completely. She got a serious disease called polio and had to remain in bed for nine months. The disease made her left leg shorter than her right, so she had serious problems walking.

When Frida was 15, she was enrolled at a prestigious school in Mexico City. There she was influenced by the modern changes that were sweeping across Mexico. She cut her hair short like a boy and started riding a bicycle—shocking for a young woman of her time. She was very interested in science and decided to become a doctor.

Then, in September 1925, Frida was involved in a horrendous accident. She was riding on a bus when it crashed into a trolley car. Her right leg was broken in 11 places, and she had many other broken bones. For the rest of her life, she had severe pain every day caused by that accident. She had to give up her plans to become a doctor, because she knew she would never be strong enough. While lying in bed after the accident, Frida began reading books about art. Her father was a painter and photographer, and he encouraged her interest in art. One year later, she completed her first painting: a portrait of herself.

Over the years, Frida Kahlo painted more than 200 pictures. Most of them were about very personal subjects—her health and her dreams. She also used many bright colors and symbols from Mexican culture.

In 1929, Frida married the famous Mexican artist Diego Rivera; they had a very difficult marriage, but she continued to paint, even after her health started failing. When a famous gallery wanted to have a show of her work, her bed was carried into the gallery so that she could talk to visitors.

Frida died in 1954, at the age of 47, but her paintings still fascinate people. In 2002, a popular movie was made of her life.

A Look at the underlined words in the reading and try to guess their meanings. Match them to the definitions.

1. biographies ___
2. remain ___
3. sweeping ___
4. horrendous ___
5. severe ___
6. encourage ___

a. extremely bad
b. moving very fast
c. very strong
d. stay
e. support and help
f. stories of people's lives

B Circle **T** for *true* or **F** for *false*.

1.	Frida Kahlo had a happy childhood until she was six.	T	F
2.	As a teenager, Frida liked modern ideas.	T	F
3.	Frida became a doctor.	T	F
4.	Frida began painting after she suffered a terrible accident.	T	F
5.	Frida's father and husband were artists, too.	T	F
6.	All of Frida's paintings were about Mexican culture.	T	F
7.	Frida had to stop painting when her health became worse.	T	F
8.	Frida died when she was still young.	T	F

C Describe the painting on the previous page. Do you like it? Explain your reasons. Where would you put it? Why?

___

___

___

___

___

___

___

___

___

UNIT 6

Review

A Solve the crossword puzzle with vocabulary and grammar from this unit.

Across

1. this material breaks if it falls
5. be a symbol for something
7. pictures on a flat surface made with paint
10. a way to do something
12. art made with only shapes and lines
13. show someone or something in a work of art
14. That pot is made of _______.
17. with a lot of variety
18. I know an artist _______ makes big sculptures.
19. a way of making art that is used by one artist

Down

2. knowing that something exists; conscious of something
3. Those shoes are made of _______.
4. Sculptures can be made of metal or _______.
6. looks like something real
8. art made from solid materials such as stone or metal
9. Clothing, curtains, and blankets are made of _______.
11. She said he _______ (win) a prize for his art. (2 words)
15. A lot of jewelry is made of this metal.
16. I want a painting _______ makes me smile.

B Circle the correct words to complete the paragraph.

I like art (1) (that | who) makes you feel good, like a (2) (clay | painting) that (3) (depicts | aware) a happy moment or a sculpture that (4) (diverse | represents) love or peace. I don't like some of the (5) (textiles | techniques) artists use in (6) (abstract | realistic) paintings. When there are only lines and shapes, I don't understand what it is. I guess I prefer (7) (abstract | realistic) art. I also really like handmade crafts, like (8) (leather | wood) bags and (9) (textiles | silver) jewelry. I always enjoy going to arts and crafts fairs.

GETTING AROUND

UNIT 7

Lesson A GRAMMAR AND VOCABULARY

A Complete the sentences with the correct form of the words in the box.

passenger vehicle fuel directly pilot reduce destination speed efficient

1. The new planes are very large. They can carry more than 700 __________.
2. This flight doesn't make any stops. It goes __________ from Singapore to London.
3. Today, long-distance flights have several __________. One of them flies the plane while the others are resting.
4. Traffic congestion is a problem in many cities because there are so many __________ on the roads.
5. Plane tickets are more expensive now because the cost of __________ for the airplanes has gone up.
6. My car is very __________. It doesn't use a lot of gasoline.
7. The __________ of flight 972 is Buenos Aires.
8. Most airplanes fly at a __________ of more than 600 kilometers per hour.
9. Faster planes will __________ the time it takes to travel from Australia to Europe.

B Write passive sentences with the present perfect tense about these developments in transportation.

1. smaller, more efficient cars/design
   Smaller and more efficient cars have been designed.
2. new kinds of fuel from plants/test __________
3. faster public transportation/plan __________
4. electric buses/develop __________
5. cars that use hydrogen/invent __________

C Read the mayor's speech. Complete the passive sentences with the present continuous tense.

Our city's transportation future *is being planned* (plan) right now. To connect us with the world, a larger airport __________ (build). Work __________ (start) on a new subway system. We have already bought hundreds of new, modern buses, and they __________ (use) by our citizens every day. And changes __________ (made) in our street system to make traffic flow better. Every day, our transportation system __________ (improve) so that the people of our city can get around more quickly and comfortably.

Lesson B GRAMMAR AND VOCABULARY

A Read the information.

National University is very crowded, so a new campus is being built 20 miles (30 kilometers) outside of the city. Nearly all of the 20,000 students live in the city. Now, there is only one small road between the city and the new campus. People have written letters to the editor about different plans for solving the transportation problem.

> The solution is simple: build a big expressway to the new campus. If 20,000 students try to drive on that small road, there will be a traffic jam all day. An expressway would cost $20 million, but other people will use it, too. The city could expand and be less crowded.

> I think the government should lend money to students to buy cheap cars. That would be good for the economy, because car dealers will sell a lot of cars. It will also be good for the students, because they will have the freedom to come and go whenever they want.

> The best idea is to build a subway line to the campus. It's true that this will take five years and cost $30 million, but subways are the fastest and most comfortable way to get around. Students work hard—we should try to make their lives easier!

> The quickest and best solution is to start a bus system from the old campus to the new campus. It's much less expensive than other plans, and we could start today. Buses aren't as fast as cars, but they save a lot of energy. Besides, students could do their homework on the bus.

B Complete the chart with information from the letters to the editor and your own ideas.

build an expressway	Advantages: Disadvantages:
lend money for cars	Advantages: Disadvantages:
build a subway	Advantages: Disadvantages:
start a bus system	Advantages: Disadvantages:

C In your opinion, which is the best plan? Explain your reasons.

____

____

____

____

Lesson C GRAMMAR AND VOCABULARY

A Match these public transportation words with their meanings.

1. board ____
2. pass ____
3. ticket ____
4. fare ____
5. route ____
6. transfer ____
7. terminal ____

a. get on a bus, train, or subway
b. the place where a bus or train line ends
c. the money that you pay to use public transportation once
d. a card that lets you use public transportation for a week or a month
e. the path traveled between two places
f. change from one bus or train to another
g. a paper that lets you use public transportation once

B Rewrite these questions to make them more polite.

1. Where is the director's office? (can you tell me)

   ____

2. What time is it? (do you know)

   ____

3. When will the doctor see me? (I'd like to know)

   ____

4. Can I use my cell phone here? (could you please tell me)

   ____

5. Is there a post office near here? (do you know)

   ____

C Complete the conversation with polite questions.

Beth: Excuse me. I want to go to the Louvre Museum. ______________?

Sylvie: Yes. From here, you take the subway to the Pont Neuf station. You have to transfer at Châtelet station.

Beth: ______________________ is close to the museum?

Sylvie: Yes, it's very close. You only have to walk for a few minutes.

Beth: ______________________________?

Sylvie: I think it costs 1 euro, but I'm not sure.

Beth: Thanks so much for your help.

Sylvie: You're welcome. Enjoy your visit.

Streets for People

Walking is the oldest way of getting around—and still one of the most important. For short distances, for exercise, or just for fun, walking is much better than driving or riding. But in many cities today, walking can also be dangerous. Cars and trucks pass much too close to pedestrians, and there are frequent accidents.

A man from Brisbane, Australia, named David Engwicht wants to do something about this. His book *Reclaiming Our Cities and Towns* has a simple message: We need to take back our streets and make them better for walking.

In the past, Engwicht says, streets belonged to everybody. Kids played there, and people walked to work or shops. Now, however, streets are designed only for cars and trucks. People stay inside to get away from the noise and dangerous traffic, and lose contact with their neighbors. Engwicht believes that people need to take back their streets.

This process is happening already in cities around the world. Neighbors in the city of Delft, in the Netherlands, took action against dangerous traffic on their street. They put old couches, tables, and other furniture in the street. Cars could still pass, but they had to drive very slowly. When the police arrived, they saw that these illegal actions were actually making the streets safer. Soon city officials started planning ways to make cars slow down and "calm" the traffic.

In many different countries, people are speaking up and working hard to make their cities safer and more pleasant for pedestrians. Cities have painted crosswalks on their streets, made streets narrower, put in traffic lights and bicycle lanes, and made plans to help more kids walk or bike to school.

Engwicht travels around the world, helping people think differently about pedestrians, streets, and neighborhoods. Besides his books and articles, he gives many speeches. He has worked in neighborhoods from Honolulu to Scotland.

Engwicht says we should think about streets as our "outdoor living room." Calming the traffic is just the beginning. In the future, streets will be safe places for children again, and walking will be more practical—and more fun.

A Match the underlined words in the reading with their meanings.

1. a place where people can walk across a street safely ________________
2. people who are walking ________________
3. make something more slow and careful ________________
4. a part of the street only for bicycles ________________
5. against the law ________________

B Circle **T** for *true* or **F** for *false*.

1. David Engwicht wrote a book about why walking is healthy. T F
2. David Engwicht thinks that people are more important than cars. T F
3. The people in Delft made it easier for pedestrians to use the streets. T F
4. The police in Delft didn't like the changes in the street. T F
5. Many cities are trying to make streets better for pedestrians. T F

C What would Engwicht think about these ideas?

1. make special streets only for pedestrians
   good idea bad idea
2. form groups for children to walk to school together
   good idea bad idea
3. build wider streets
   good idea bad idea
4. make cars drive slower on all city streets
   good idea bad idea
5. put more parking lots in the city
   good idea bad idea

D Write about walking in your city. Is it a good place for walking? Why or why not? How many people walk there? What changes would make your city better for walking?

____

____

____

____

____

UNIT 7

Review

A Solve the crossword puzzle with vocabulary and grammar from this unit.

Across

2. the place where a bus or train is going
3. The _______ for the subway is $1.
5. a person who is traveling on a train, bus, etc.
7. Electric cars (make) _______ today. (3 words)
9. You buy this to take a trip on public transportation.
10. (know) _______ how much a ticket costs? (3 words)
14. change from one bus or train to another
16. (tell) _______ me where the bus stop is? (3 words)

Down

1. Three new airports (build) _______ in the last 10 years. (3 words)
4. the way a bus or train goes to a place
5. a person whose job is flying airplanes
6. the end of a bus or train line
8. without stopping
11. a substance like gasoline or oil
12. A bus _______ for one month costs $20.
13. get on a plane or train
15. how fast you are going

B Circle the correct words to complete the paragraph.

In many cities around the world, city councils want to (1) (transfer | reduce) the number of (2) (vehicles | passengers) on the streets, so public transportation is (3) (been improved | being improved) to make it more (4) (directly | efficient) and attractive to travelers. Buses and trains have (5) (been designed | being designed) to use less (6) (fuel | fare), and better bus (7) (destinations | terminals) are (8) (being built | been built). In most big cities, (9) (tickets | passengers) can buy a weekly or monthly (10) (pass | transfer), which means they can use buses and trains without buying a (11) (ticket | board) every time they want to ride, and it makes the (12) (fuel | fare) cheaper for them.

COMPETITION

UNIT 8

Lesson A GRAMMAR AND VOCABULARY

A Complete the sentences with the correct form of the words in the box.

athlete match training competitive game individual win lose team sportsmanship

1. At the Olympics, ____________________ from every country in the world come together to compete.
2. Yoshi plays on his university's soccer ____________________.
3. Some of the runners stopped to help another runner when she fell during the race. That's an example of good ____________________!
4. At the Olympics, when you ____________________ a competition, you get a gold medal.
5. It was a very exciting tennis ____________________. Both of the women played really well.
6. Athletes need many years of ____________________ before they can compete in the Olympics.
7. In ____________________ sports, there is usually a winner and a loser.
8. I ____________________ the big tennis match, so I decided to practice harder every week.
9. The soccer ____________________ was excellent; both teams played really well.
10. Some people prefer ____________________ sports; others prefer sports you play with a team.

B Complete the conversations with the negative questions at right.

Shouldn't you call your parents?

Aren't you tired?

Don't you want to go out to dinner?

Isn't your friend a nurse?

Don't you like chocolate?

1. ____
   Yes, I am. I started work at 4:00 a.m. today.
2. ____
   No. She's actually a doctor.
3. ____
   No, not really. It's too sweet for me.
4. ____
   No, I don't. I want to stay home and have a quiet evening.
5. ____
   Yes. I'll talk to them tonight.

C Answer these negative questions.

1. Aren't you American? ____
2. Weren't you late for class yesterday? ____
3. Don't you like sports? ____
4. Shouldn't you save more money? ____

Lesson B GRAMMAR AND VOCABULARY

A Unscramble the names of sports.

1. bbaallse ______________
2. tindabnom ______________
3. intsne ______________
4. inskig ______________
5. ratmila star ______________
6. ofgl ______________
7. erccos ______________
8. glicybinc ______________
9. lolelylavb ______________
10. noxbig ______________
11. skallbetab ______________
12. wgmismin ______________

B Read these people's answers on the questionnaire. Then choose the best sport for each one, and explain your reasons.

Sport Preference Questionnaire

Name: *Danny Santos*

1. Which kinds of exercise do you prefer—vigorous or gentle? *Both kinds are OK. But I want to play a sport to help me relax after classes.*
2. Are you an introvert or an extrovert? *It depends. I like to spend time with a few good friends, but I also like to be alone a lot.*
3. Are you a perfectionist? *Yes, but I try not to get upset when I make a mistake.*
4. Are you very focused when you do things? *I have to be very focused—I'm a chemistry major at the university.*
5. Do you like to do one thing, or do you prefer a lot of change? *I prefer to do one thing at a time.*

The best sport for Danny is ______________.

Reasons: ______________

____

____

____

Sport Preference Questionnaire

Name: *LaKeisha Green*

1. Which kinds of exercise do you prefer—vigorous or gentle? *I sit at a desk all day at work, so I like to really move during my free time!*
2. Are you an introvert or an extrovert? *Definitely an extrovert. I get bored when I'm alone.*
3. Are you a perfectionist? *Not really. And when I play sports, I want to have fun.*
4. Are you very focused when you do things? *I can be when I'm at work. But it's nice to have a break from that.*
5. Do you like to do one thing, or do you prefer a lot of change? *I really like to do a lot of different things.*

The best sport for LaKeisha is ______________.

Reasons: ______________

____

____

____

Lesson C GRAMMAR AND VOCABULARY

A Read the newspaper article and fill in the spaces with words from the box.

points coach championship score medal trophy scoreboard

Metro City Wins In Youth Soccer Tournament

Metro City won the National Youth Soccer league yesterday when they defeated Southland with a (1)_______________ of 4-2. It was a very close and exciting game, with 2 (2)_______________ scored in the last five minutes. "I am so proud of every member of the team," said their (3)_______________, Jesse Curtis. "All of the players worked tremendously hard all year to get to, and win, the (4)_______________." Each player received a gold (5)_______________ from the president, and the team was awarded a large (6)_______________ with all their names on it. At the end of the award ceremony, the (7)_______________ showed the words "Metro is #1" and the whole audience cheered.

B Fill in a relative pronoun in each sentence.

1. The man _______________ I met at the party is from South Africa.
2. Did you eat the cake _______________ I brought home?
3. The book _______________ we had to read for our class was 400 pages long!
4. The actor _______________ I like the most is Matt Damon.
5. My mother really enjoyed the presents _______________ we gave her.

C Combine the two sentences by writing an adjective clause.

1. He bought a car. The car was very expensive.
   The car that he bought was very expensive.
2. We watched a movie. The movie was more than three hours long.
   ____
3. The teacher asked me a question. I couldn't answer the question.
   ____
4. He told me the news. The news was good.
   ____
5. I saw the thieves. The thieves were wearing black clothes.
   ____

Voice Your Opinion:

Change Is Needed in Youth Sports

by Richard Wade

Everywhere you look, you see kids bouncing a basketball or waving a tennis racket. And these kids are getting younger and younger. In this country, children can compete on basketball, baseball, and volleyball teams starting at age nine. The youth soccer organization has teams for children as young as five. And swimming and gymnastics classes begin at age four, to prepare children for competition.

It's true that a few of these kids will develop into highly skilled athletes and may even become members of our national Olympic teams. But what about the others—the average kids? This emphasis on competition in sports is having serious negative effects.

Children who get involved in competitive sports at a young age often grow tired of their sport. Many parents pressure their kids to choose one sport and devote all their time to it. A survey found that 79 percent of parents of young athletes wanted their children to concentrate on one sport. But 66 percent of the young athletes wanted to play more than one sport—for fun.

Another problem is the pressure imposed by over-competitive parents and coaches. Children are not naturally competitive. In fact, a recent study by Paulo David found that most children don't even understand the idea of competition until they are seven years old. Very young kids don't know why their parents are pushing them so hard.

The third, and biggest, problem for young athletes is the lack of time to do their homework, have fun, be with friends—in short, time to be kids. When they are forced to spend every afternoon at sports practice, they often start to hate their chosen sport. Researchers found that 70 percent of kids who take part in competitive sports before the age of twelve quit before they turn eighteen. Many of them completely lose interest in sports. Excessive competition takes away all the enjoyment.

We need to remember the purpose of youth sports—to give kids a chance to have fun while developing strong, healthy bodies.

A What is the main idea of this reading?

a. many children in this country spend too much time playing sports

b. sports for children have two important purposes

c. too much competition is not good for children

B Find the information in the reading.

1. The age when children can start these sports:

a. swimming ______ **c.** basketball ______

b. soccer ______ **d.** gymnastics ______

2. The number of children who want to play more than one sport: ______ percent

3. The number of children who stop playing their sport before they are eighteen: ______ percent

4. The age when children understand the idea of competition: ______

5. The number of parents who want their children to play only one sport: ______ percent

6. Three problems with youth sports that the author describes:

a. ______________________

b. ______________________

c. ______________________

7. The two purposes of youth sports that the author mentions:

a. ______________________

b. ______________________

C Are competitive sports good or bad for children under sixteen? Give your opinion, and explain with examples and reasons.

____

____

____

____

____

____

____

____

____

UNIT 8

Review

A Solve the crossword puzzle with vocabulary and grammar from this unit.

Across

1. a group of people who play a sport together
4. The book _______ I read was interesting.
7. She won a gold _______ at the Olympics last year.
8. being polite while you are playing a sport
11. The teacher _______ I like the most is Dr. Kim.
12. the opposite of win
13. The _______ of the basketball game was 67–59.
14. The boots _______ I bought were made in Argentina.

Down

1. learning and practicing a sport
2. He scored four _______ for his team.
3. a competition to find the best player or team in a sport
5. someone who plays a sport
6. a person who trains athletes
8. Look at the _______ to see how many points each team has.
9. a big cup for the winner of a competition
10. The tennis _______ was really exciting!
14. When you do better than the other athletes, you _______.

B Complete the paragraph with the words in the box.

boxing	match	coach	competitive	individual	championship	win	training	athletes	swimming

I'm a professional boxer, so (1) ____________________ is an important part of my routine. My (2) ____________________ and I meet every morning, and I have to run, jump rope, and practice boxing moves and strategies. I usually have a (3) ____________________ against a training partner, too, but it's not (4) ____________________; it is only to help us both practice. When I participate in the (5) ____________________, I am really competitive! All (6) ____________________ like to (7) ____________________. They want to be the best, don't they? I am very serious about (8) ____________________. I do other sports for fun; I like (9) ____________________ and golf to relax. I guess I prefer (10) ____________________ sports; I don't really like playing on a team!

DANGER

Lesson A GRAMMAR AND VOCABULARY

A Complete the advertisement with the correct form of the words in the box.

estimate poison risk survive substance toxic injured prevent

Safe at Home?

The government ____________ that more than 12,000 children in this country had accidents at home last year. The ____________ is highest for children under the age of five.

One of the most common household accidents is eating or drinking ____________. Many of our common cleaning products contain ____________ that are ____________, especially to very small children. And every year, many children are ____________ when they play with scissors, knives, or cigarette lighters.

Look at your house through your children's eyes, and put dangerous items in a place that kids can't reach. Keep your doctor's phone number in a place that's easy to find. Children can ____________ even serious accidents if they are treated quickly.

For simple ideas on how you can ____________ accidents and keep your children safe, please visit our Web site.

B Match the sentences to the tag questions.

1. John doesn't like cats, _____
2. You don't know the answer, _____
3. He's coming to the party, _____
4. Markus isn't in the office today, _____
5. You're not going to wear that T-shirt, _____
6. Alan got a new job, _____
7. Risa lives in Tokyo, _____
8. Nicholas was late for class, _____

a. isn't he?
b. do you?
c. are you?
d. wasn't he?
e. doesn't she?
f. is he?
g. didn't he?
h. does he?

C Add a tag question to the sentences.

1. That kind of snake is dangerous, ____________?
2. Some cleaning products are toxic, ____________?
3. He wasn't injured in the accident, ____________?
4. You hurt yourself, ____________?
5. Many accidents at home can be prevented, ____________?

Lesson B GRAMMAR AND VOCABULARY

A Complete the chart about these dangerous jobs. Use your own knowledge and ideas.

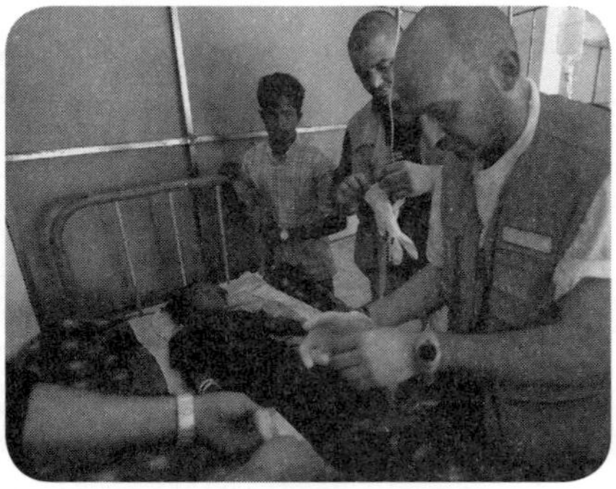

Job	Reasons why someone would want to do this job	Reasons why this job is dangerous
Logger	*You can work outdoors*	*You might fall from a tree*
Disaster relief worker		
Police officer		

B Choose one of these jobs and think of a friend, family member, or classmate who would be good at it. Write about why it is a good job for that person.

____

____

____

____

____

____

____

____

Lesson C GRAMMAR AND VOCABULARY

A Read each situation and fill in the blank with a sentence from the box.

Where's the nearest pharmacy?	Where's the emergency room?
Where's the nearest hospital?	Call an ambulance!
Call the fire department!	Call the police!

1. You work in a jewelry store. A thief runs out the door with an expensive watch. You say, "____________________"
2. You have a very bad cold and you want to buy some medicine. You say, "____________________"
3. You're at the hospital and you need to find the place where people can see a doctor very quickly. You say, "____________________"
4. You see smoke coming from a window in your school. You say, "____________________"
5. You are driving and you have a car accident. A woman in the other car has a bad cut and can't walk. You say, "____________________"
6. Your friend has pain in his stomach and you want to take him to a clinic. You say, "____________________"

B Choose the correct word to complete each adverbial clause.

1. (As soon as | Before) I saw the smoke, I left the building.
2. Don't forget to lock the door (whenever | before) you leave the house. You have to do it every time.
3. I always take a bath (before | as soon as) I go to bed.
4. (Whenever | After) Marta called an ambulance, she tried to help the injured man.
5. (After | When) you walk in the mountains, you should watch carefully for snakes.

C What do you do at these times? Write sentences with adverbial clauses of time.

1. as soon as you get home *As soon as I get home, I . . .*
2. before you go to bed ____________________
3. after you finish studying ____________________
4. whenever you have free time ____________________
5. when you want to have fun with your friends ____________________

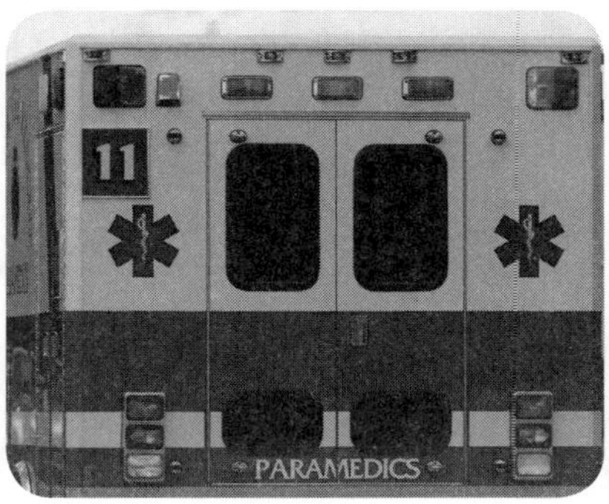

Lesson D READING AND WRITING

Your Turn: Should Risky Sports Be Banned?

A team of mountain climbers wanted to be the first to climb a particular mountain in the winter. Then they had to be rescued by army helicopters. Nearly a hundred sailboats were participating in an ocean race when a severe storm occurred. Two sailors and one rescue worker died during the rescue mission. Adventurer Richard Branson tried to fly a balloon around the world and crashed several times. Millions of dollars were spent to search for him and bring him home safely. We asked our readers for their opinions.

Paulo: What, exactly, is a risky sport? People have died while swimming, playing soccer, or even walking, but no one says those sports are dangerous. I could get in an accident while driving to my office. You can't ban all risky sports, because people have different definitions of "risky."

Jackie: Yes, they should be banned! Why should these risk takers put other people's lives in danger? And why should citizens pay all that tax money for rescue operations? Public money should not be used to help people who get into trouble with risky sports. They should be free to take any risks they want, but only if they plan ahead for rescue if they need it.

Matt: It is a personal choice to put your life at risk. We should not allow the government to put limits on our lives. If you are an adult, it should be your decision, not the government's! And if rescuers have decided to take a dangerous job, that was their choice, too. The world would be very boring if people never took risks.

Lisa: All people need a challenge. Some people really enjoy taking risks, and if high-risk sports are banned, they will feel unhappy and look for risky adventures in other areas, like business or politics, or their personal life. That would cause a lot more problems in the world.

Ramesh: They should be banned, and journalists should stop writing and talking about the things that these crazy people do. All this publicity gives a lot of bad ideas to teenagers and encourages them to try dangerous things.

A Circle **T** for *true* or **F** for *false*.

1.	According to the article, there have been many sports accidents recently.	T	F
2.	Paulo thinks people disagree about which sports are risky.	T	F
3.	Jackie wants to spend more money to help people do risky sports.	T	F
4.	Richard Branson had several accidents while flying in his balloon.	T	F
5.	Matt thinks the government should make more rules to keep people safe.	T	F
6.	Lisa thinks that risky sports are good for some people.	T	F
7.	Ramesh thinks that news articles about risky sports make teenagers want to try them.	T	F
8.	All of these readers want to ban risky sports.	T	F
9.	Lisa thinks that banning risky sports could make people take other risks.	T	F

B Find examples of these things in the article. Then add more examples of your own.

Risky sports
Sports that people think are safe
Other kinds of risks that people take

C Write a paragraph giving your opinion about risky sports. Be sure to give examples and reasons.

UNIT 9

Review

A Solve the crossword puzzle with vocabulary and grammar from this unit.

Across

2. I go to a movie _______ I have time.
5. He wasn't there, _______? (2 words)
7. His leg was _______ in a car accident.
9. stop from happening
10. If you see smoke in a building, you should call the fire _______.
12. containing poison
13. a place to buy medicine
15. Where's the _______ hospital?
16. You live in Buenos Aires, _______? (2 words)
17. guess about a number

Down

1. live through a dangerous experience
3. If you need to see a doctor quickly, go to the _______ room in the hospital.
4. It's dangerous, _______? (2 words)
6. a solid, liquid, or gas
8. They're Korean, _______? (2 words)
11. An _______ will take you to the hospital.
13. something that will kill you if you eat it
14. possibility that something bad will happen

B Complete the paragraph with words from the box.

before	as soon as	risks	nearest	prevented	whenever	ambulance	substances	injured	before

Both children and adults are often (1) _________________ in their own home because of accidents that could be (2) _________________. There are always (3) _________________ in life. Accidents happen at home, driving your car, playing a sport, and in many other situations. It is important to take action (4) _________________ something happens; for example, call an (5) _________________ or the fire department or find the (6) _________________ hospital. But it is also important to try to prevent accidents (7) _________________ they happen. For example, (8) _________________ you are going on a trip in your car, you should get the car checked (9) _________________ you leave. At home, make sure toxic (10) _________________ cannot be reached by children. Prevention is the best cure.

MYSTERIES

UNIT 10

Lesson A GRAMMAR AND VOCABULARY

A Complete the sentences with the correct form of the words in the box.

carve	remains	speculate	prehistoric
figure out	massive	evidence	investigations

1. Scientists have found ____________________ that shows that the first people in our country sailed here in small wooden boats.
2. A team of scientists will ____________________ the kinds of tools that were used to ____________________ the stone Olmec heads in Mexico.
3. There have been many ____________________ to try to find out how the huge stones for the heads were moved.
4. The Olmec heads are ____________________. The smallest weighs 6 tons and the largest is estimated to weigh about 45 tons.
5. Along with the people in the old tombs, archaeologists found the ____________________ of horses, dogs, and other kinds of animals that lived at the time.
6. We don't know exactly what happened to Amelia Earhart when she was flying across the Pacific. Some people ____________________ that she landed on a small island.
7. Archaeologists have learned a lot about ____________________ people by studying their tools, food, and weapons.

B Write sentences speculating about each situation. Use the verb in parentheses.

1. Sunny got 90 percent on her vocabulary test. (must) ____________________
____
2. I left a plate of cookies on the table, and now it's not there. (may) ________
____
3. Leo just checked his e-mail, and now he's smiling. (might) ______________
____
4. It's time for class, but our teacher isn't here. (could) ________________
____
5. Nancy looks really tired today. (must) ____________________
____

C Look at the picture. How did ancient people make this building? Write sentences in your notebook speculating with *may have, might have, must have*, or *could have*.

Lesson B GRAMMAR AND VOCABULARY

A Read the information about a mystery and answer the questions.

One of the world's strangest mysteries is a monster called the *chupacabra*. Some people say this animal has killed more than 2,000 farm animals in Puerto Rico in recent years, such as chickens, rabbits, dogs, and even horses. The dead animals have deep holes in their necks. Often, much of their blood has been removed, but there is no blood on the ground.

Many of the attacks have occurred in an area of Puerto Rico called El Yunque, a jungle that is a national park. Much of Puerto Rico is dense jungle, which could be the home of unknown animals. Similar attacks have been reported in Costa Rica, Nicaragua, Mexico, and Brazil.

A few people say that they have seen a chupacabra. They describe an animal about one meter tall, covered in brown hair, and walking on two legs. Its legs are thick and strong, but the upper part of its body is small. Other people say that the chupacabra is just a fantasy and that the animals' deaths have a natural explanation.

1. Do you think the chupacabra could be real? Explain your answer.

____

____

2. How could people prove that the chupacabra is real or not real?

____

____

3. Should scientists try to find out the truth about the chupacabra? Why or why not?

____

____

What happened to Amelia Earhart?

Why were the Nazca lines made?

Are UFOs real?

How did the Egyptians make the pyramids?

Is there a monster in Loch Ness?

B Which of the mysteries in the box would you most like to know the answer to? Circle it and explain your reasons.

____

____

____

____

____

____

____

Lesson C GRAMMAR AND VOCABULARY

A Unscramble the expressions for showing surprise. Add capital letters and punctuation.

1. ttash zamniga ____________________
2. laryel ____________________
3. ryueo dikgind ____________________
4. blkarmaere ____________________
5. oww ____________________

B Jessie had a lot of plans for the weekend, but she didn't do them. Write about her plans and what she did instead. Use the future in the past tense and the simple past tense.

1. Jessie was ____________________
2. Instead, she ____________________
3. ____________________
4. ____________________
5. ____________________
6. ____________________
7. ____________________
8. ____________________

C Write about three things that you planned to do during your last vacation but didn't do. Use the future in the past tense and the simple past tense.

1. Your plan: ____________________

   What you really did: ____________________
2. Your plan: ____________________

   What you really did: ____________________
3. Your plan: ____________________

   What you really did: ____________________

Lesson D READING AND WRITING

The Mysteries of Nazca

In the desert of Peru, 300 kilometers from Lima, one of the most unusual artworks in the world has mystified people for decades. Seen from the ground, it looks like lines scratched into the earth. But from high above, these marks are huge images of birds, fish, and seashells, all beautifully carved into the earth.

The Nazca lines are so difficult to see from the ground that they weren't discovered until the 1930s, when pilots spotted them while flying over the area. In all, there are about 70 different human and animal figures on the plain, along with 900 triangles, circles, and lines.

Researchers have figured out that the lines are at least 1,500 years old, but their purpose is still a mystery. A Swiss writer named Erich von Däniken wrote that the Nazca lines were designed as a landing place for UFOs. However, it would probably be very tricky to land a spaceship in the middle of pictures of dogs and monkeys.

In the 1940s, an American explorer named Paul Kosok suggested that the drawings were a chronicle of the movement of the stars and planets. He called Nazca "the largest astronomy book in the world." Later, an astronomer tested his theory with a computer, but he couldn't find any relation between the lines and movements in space.

Another explanation is that the lines may have been made for religious reasons. British researcher Tony Morrison investigated the customs of people in the Andes Mountains and learned that they sometimes pray by the side of the road. It's possible that in the past, the lines of Nazca were created for a similar purpose. The largest pictures may have been the sites for special ceremonies. But the local people have never constructed anything this big.

Recently, two other scientists, David Johnson and Steve Mabee, have speculated that the lines could have been related to water. Nazca is one of the driest places in the world and receives only 2 cm of rain every year. While Johnson was searching for ancient water sources in the area, he noticed that some waterways built by ancient people were connected with the lines. Johnson believes that the Nazca lines are a giant map of the underground water in the area. Other scientists are now searching for evidence to prove this.

A Read the article and complete the chart.

Person	Theory	Evidence for or against this theory
Erich von Däniken	*The Nazca lines are* ______ ______	
Paul Kosok		
Tony Morrison		
David Johnson Steve Mabee		

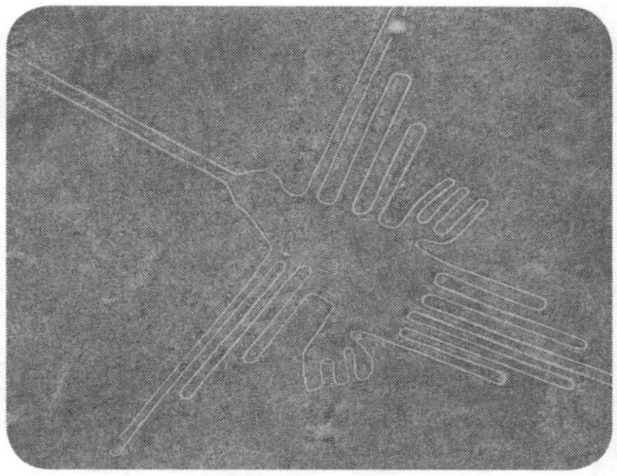

B Look at the underlined words in the reading and try to guess their meaning without using your dictionary.

1. *Spotted* probably means ______.
   a. saw b. crashed into c. made
2. *Tricky* probably means ______.
   a. interesting b. easy c. difficult
3. A *chronicle* probably means ______.
   a. a speculation b. a history c. a theory
4. *Waterway* probably means ______.
   a. something to drink b. a kind of pot c. a narrow place that carries water

C Is it important to find the answers to mysteries like this? Why or why not?

____

____

____

____

____

Review

A Solve the crossword puzzle with vocabulary and grammar from this unit.

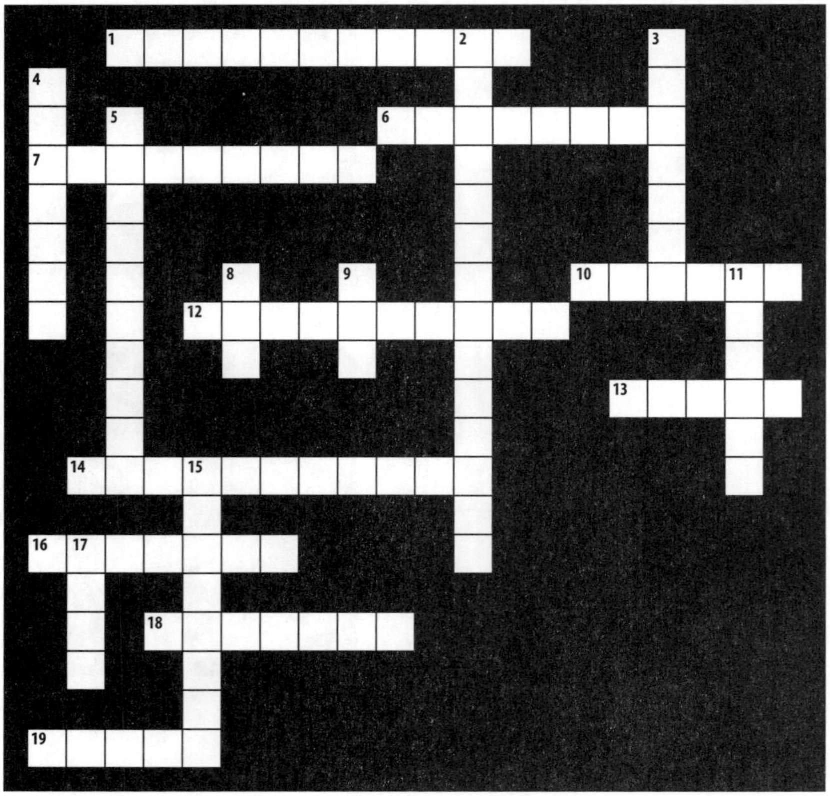

Across

1. before written history
6. showed
7. guess about something
10. Scientists are trying to _______ out how people moved the stones.
12. I _______ be an actor when I grew up. (3 words)
13. UFOs _______ have landed in the desert without people seeing them.
14. We _______ do our homework last night, but we watched a movie instead. (3 words)
16. "The Pyramids in Egypt are more than 6,000 years old." "That's _______!"
18. the parts of something that are left after the rest of it is gone
19. shape stone, wood, or other hard materials using sharp objects

Down

2. research; studies
3. "I saw a sea monster." "You're _______!"
4. huge
5. very surprising
8. People from other planets _______ have visited Earth.
9. You say this when you are surprised.
11. "I saw a chupacabra." "_______?"
15. clues that show something is true
17. Jason isn't in class today. He _______ be sick.

B Complete the paragraph with words from the box.

may have been	investigations	could have
prehistoric	remains	must have been
massive	figure out	speculate	evidence

Stonehenge is a (1) _______________ monument in England. Nobody knows exactly how or why it was built, but a lot of people (2) _______________. Some people believe that aliens (3) _______________ made it; others are certain that it (4) _______________ a religious place. There have been a lot of (5) _______________ as archaeologists try to (6) _______________ how the (7) _______________ stones were moved and what Stonehenge really was. Human (8) _______________ have been found at the site, and some archaeologists now think that it (9) _______________ a place where sick people came to be healed, but there is not enough (10) _______________ for them to be sure.

LEARNING

Lesson A GRAMMAR AND VOCABULARY

A Complete the advertisement with words from the box.

semester campus courses tuition scholarships apply requirement deadline

Living English, every day!

Living English is an exciting four-month __________ in the United States and Canada. Students live on the __________ of a local university and take special __________ in North American history, literature, and culture, along with English classes in small groups. We have programs in Seattle, Miami, or Toronto; one of them is perfect for you!

Students in any field can __________ to this program and experience life in North America, but intermediate level English is a __________. The __________ for this program is $3,000, but we have __________ available to help you pay for the cost.

The __________ to enroll is March 1st.

For more information, please visit our Web site.

B Write answers to these people. Use *should (not) have, could have,* or *would have* and the verb in parentheses.

1. **Your friend:** I watched movies until 2:00 a.m. Now I'm really tired.
   You: (go to bed) __________.
2. **Your friend:** I didn't eat lunch because I left my wallet at home.
   You: (lend) __________.
3. **Your friend:** I'm sorry you had to wait for me for an hour. My car broke down.
   You: (call) __________.
4. **Your friend:** I'm really upset. I've gained ten kilos this year!
   You: (eat) __________.
5. **Your friend:** Our teacher looks angry with me. I wonder why?
   You: (do) __________.
6. **Your friend:** I spent ten hours cleaning my apartment because my parents are coming to visit.
   You: (call) __________.

C Write sentences about these things with *should (not) have, could have,* or *would have.*

1. a mistake you made __________
2. something you didn't try __________
3. something you wish you had done __________

Lesson B GRAMMAR AND VOCABULARY

A Fill in the name of the learning style.

Auditory Visual Kinesthetic Reading/Writing

1. ____________ learners like to use their eyes to take in information.
2. ____________ learners use printed words to get new information.
3. ____________ learners take in information by using their bodies.
4. ____________ learners like to get new information by hearing it.

B Read what these people say about their experiences. What is each person's learning style?

1. **Alicia says:** "I tried to learn Chinese once, but I didn't get very far. The lessons just weren't right for me. The teacher was really nice—she was from Beijing—and she was going to teach me conversation. She said that writing Chinese is difficult, so it's better to just learn speaking. Well, we practiced all kinds of sentences, but I could never remember them. I forgot them as soon as she said them. To remember things, I really need to see them written down. Next time, I want to take a class that uses a textbook."

   Alicia is a/an ____________ learner.

2. **Brandon says:** "I had so many problems in school when I was younger! It was hard for me to sit at a desk all day and just listen and write. I was bored all the time, so I caused a lot of trouble for the teachers. I'm really glad that I went to a technical high school. I studied computer repair, and I finally had some interesting classes where I could use my hands to do something. Now I have a great job in an electronics store, because I learned how to do something useful."

   Brandon is a/an____________ learner.

looking at paintings / practicing a dance / attending a lecture / making a cake / using a map of Africa / reading a Web site / doing a science experiment / listening to an author read his poems / finding new words in the dictionary

C Which learning style are these activities good for? Write each activity in the chart.

Auditory	Visual
Reading/Writing	**Kinesthetic**

Lesson C GRAMMAR AND VOCABULARY

A Match the name of the major with the things students learn about.

1. economics ____	**a.** how the human mind works
2. education ____	**b.** raising food, plants, and animals
3. agriculture ____	**c.** designing machines, roads, bridges, etc.
4. law ____	**d.** how people learn
5. business ____	**e.** Earth and its rocks and minerals
6. engineering ____	**f.** how different substances react together
7. psychology ____	**g.** why companies succeed or fail
8. chemistry ____	**h.** the money system in a country
9. social work ____	**i.** helping people with family or social problems
10. geology ____	**j.** the legal system in a country

B Underline the noun clauses in these sentences.

1. What you told me was really interesting.
2. I don't remember where I bought that book.
3. In that class, students learn about how Earth and its rocks were formed.
4. Sachi can tell you how to get to the new mall.
5. I can really understand why she felt so nervous.
6. My friends told me what I should do.

C Anita and Janie are talking about their possible new roommate. Write Janie's answers using the words in parentheses and noun clauses.

1. **Anita:** Where did you meet her?
   Janie: (not remember) ________________________________
2. **Anita:** Who does she live with at the moment?
   Janie: (have no idea) ________________________________
3. **Anita:** What kind of a job does she have?
   Janie: (not sure) ________________________________
4. **Anita:** Who are her friends?
   Janie: (not know) ________________________________
5. **Anita:** When would she move in?
   Janie: (she/not tell me) ________________________________

Lesson D READING AND WRITING

Students Return from Adventure Abroad

Four students from National University have recently returned from Africa, where they participated in development projects with local residents in rural areas. For 10 weeks, these young people worked in Zimbabwe and Botswana as members of a program called Raleigh International.

Raleigh International, founded by the Prince of Wales in 1984, gives young people a chance to do volunteer work while experiencing other countries and **their** cultures. The program, named after the explorer Sir Walter Raleigh, encourages young people to help others and work in difficult settings. More than 30,000 students from a variety of cultures and backgrounds have volunteered in a total of 40 countries.

Marisa Silvestri, 20, a business major, traveled to Zimbabwe to work with a group in the Mavuradonha Wilderness Area. Their first project was helping farmers build electric fences to keep elephants from destroying **their** crops. When elephants entered the village one night, the students joined with farmers to drive **them** away and preserve the fields. Silvestri's group also constructed small cottages for tourists to stay in, built in the local style.

Saeed Mohammed, also 20 and an engineering major, joined another group in Zimbabwe. His group carried out a survey of health problems in several villages and taught children about good health habits. Saeed said the kids were so curious about the Raleigh International students that after the health lessons, they asked **them** questions about "everything else under the sun."

Saeed's group also worked to build foot trails through the forest. While they were out working in the bush, a fire broke out, destroying eight kilometers of forest. The students fought to bring the fire under control, sleeping only 45 minutes during the two days that it raged.

In Botswana, two 19-year-old students, LaKeishia Young and David Min, helped to build a clinic and a meeting hall in a small village. Though they didn't face angry elephants, they said the building work was much harder than they expected. "It was a great learning experience," Young said.

After all the hard work, the four students found time for fun. They took boat trips, learned African dances, and traveled together for a week after **their** program ended.

A Find the information in the article.

1. two countries where the students did volunteer work:

   ____________________, ____________________

2. the name of the volunteer program: ____________________
3. the year the program started: ____________________
4. the number of people who have volunteered with the program since it began: ____________________
5. five projects that the students worked on: ____________________,

   ____________________, ____________________,

   ____________________, ____________________

6. two dangerous situations that the students faced: ____________________,

   ____

7. three things that the students did to relax: ____________________,

   ____________________, ____________________

B Look back at the reading and find what each of the pronouns in **bold** refers to.

1. **their** (par. 2)
   a. Wales **b.** young people **c.** countries **d.** settings
2. **their** (par. 3)
   a. group **b.** farmers **c.** fences **d.** elephants
3. **them** (par. 3)
   a. crops **b.** students **c.** elephants **d.** farmers
4. **them** (par. 4)
   a. kids **b.** health **c.** lessons **d.** students
5. **their** (par. 7)
   a. students **b.** boats **c.** dances **d.** programs

C Write about a difficult experience that you learned something from.

____

____

____

____

____

____

____

____

UNIT 11

Review

A Solve the crossword puzzle with vocabulary and grammar from this unit.

Across

1. an area of land with university buildings
3. a series of lessons in one subject
5. the study of legal systems
6. I _______ said hello, but I didn't see you. (2 words)
7. the study of the human mind
8. the study of the earth and its rocks
11. something that you must have
13. the main subject that you are studying
17. I _______ eaten so much ice cream. It was a bad idea. (2 words)

Down

1. I _______ studied in Canada. It was possible. (2 words)
2. half of a school year
4. Andy got a _______. He got $5,000 to pay for college because he's an excellent student.
9. the study of how food is grown on farms
10. the study of designing and making buildings or machines
12. the study of money
14. money you pay for education
15. join a class or school
16. I liked _______ you said.

B Complete the paragraph with words from the box.

law tuition campus what enroll where apply scholarships major engineering deadline

After high school, some people choose to study a (1) ____________________ in college. Before you make your decision, you have to do some investigation. You need to know (2) ____________________ you want to study; for example, (3) ____________________, economics, or (4) ____________________. You also need to decide (5) ____________________ you want to study. It is a good idea to visit the (6) ____________________ before you (7) ____________________ at the university. After you have decided what to study and where, you need to find out when the (8) ____________________ to (9) ____________________ is. If you send in your application late, they won't consider you. You should also ask about (10) ____________________ to get help paying the (11) ____________________.

SPACE

Lesson A GRAMMAR AND VOCABULARY

A Complete the sentences with the correct form of the words in the box.

solar system	satellite
spacecraft	manned
unmanned	planet
space station	colonizing
mission	orbit

1. Some people think that ______________ other planets might happen in the future.
2. The first ______________ space flight was in 1961. It was made by a Russian cosmonaut named Yuri Gagarin.
3. Before Gagarin flew in space, there were other ______________ flights that carried dogs.
4. Earth and the other planets ______________ the sun.
5. The exploration of the ______________ has given us valuable information and helped to develop many important products that we use every day.
6. Venus and Mars are the ______________ closest to us.
7. The last ______________ to the moon was in 1975.
8. Today, we use ______________ for communication, observing the weather, and many other purposes.
9. Scientists and astronauts live on a ______________ for several weeks or months to learn more about space.
10. A ______________ is a vehicle which is designed to travel in space.

B Will people live on other planets in the future? Write your predictions with *will* or *going to.*

1. ______________________________________
2. ______________________________________
3. ______________________________________
4. ______________________________________

C Circle the verb forms that make correct sentences about the future. More than one answer may be correct, with different meanings.

1. The weather forecast said it ______________ tomorrow.
   a. will snow **b.** is going to snow **c.** snows **d.** is snowing
2. "We don't have any more coffee." "I ______________ to the store and get some."
   a. 'll go **b.** am going to go **c.** go **d.** am going
3. The test ______________ at 10:00 a.m.
   a. will start **b.** is going to start **c.** starts **d.** is starting
4. In the year 2020, people ______________ vacations in space.
   a. will take **b.** are going to take **c.** take **d.** are taking

Lesson B GRAMMAR AND VOCABULARY

A The government of your country has decided to send one "citizen astronaut" to spend a month at the International Space Station. Read the information and make notes about each candidate.

Lydia is a science teacher at a high school. She has always been interested in the universe, and she loves teaching students about space. She is 43 years old and has five children. Her health is good, but she can't see very well without her glasses. Reason for wanting to travel in space: "I can share my experiences with my students and young people in our country."

Positive:	Negative:

Ryan is 28 years old. He is a professional athlete and a member of the national soccer team, which did very well in the last World Cup championship. He is engaged and will marry his girlfriend next year. His health is excellent, even though he smokes cigarettes. Reason for wanting to travel in space: "All my life I have loved adventure, and space is the biggest adventure of all."

Positive:	Negative:

Jorge is a doctor at a free clinic for poor people. Many people admire his work. He is 51 years old, and his health is fair. He got very sick last year from overworking, but he feels better now. He is married, and his two children are adults. Reason for wanting to travel in space: "Exploring the universe gives us hope. I want to bring that hope to everyone on Earth."

Positive:	Negative:

B Who should be the citizen astronaut? In your notebook, write about your opinion and explain your reasons.

C Write these compound nouns correctly (one word, two words, or hyphenated). Then say them out loud.

1. space + craft ____________
2. follow + up ____________
3. back + pack ____________
4. space + station ____________
5. life + saver ____________
6. check + in ____________
7. hard + ware ____________
8. space + walk ____________
9. bed + room ____________
10. fruit + juice ____________

Lesson C GRAMMAR AND VOCABULARY

A Match the parts of these time expressions.

1. in a little ___	**a.** these days
2. someday ___	**b.** soon
3. one ___	**c.** years
4. one of ___	**d.** while
5. in ten ___	**e.** later
6. sooner or ___	**f.** day

B Write sentences about the future using *may*, *might*, or *could*.

people/start colonies on the moon ____________________

new medicines/cure cancer ____________________

astronauts/find living things on other planets ____________________

scientists/live permanently in space ____________________

new planets/be found far away in the universe ____________________

C Complete the sentences about the future with *be able to, have to,* or *need to* and the verb in parentheses.

1. My plane leaves at 6:00 a.m. I (go) ___will have to go___ to the airport very early.
2. I can play a few songs on my guitar now. After I take guitar lessons, I (play) __________ a lot of songs.
3. If people take vacations in space, they (see) __________ beautiful views of Earth.
4. My mother's birthday is on Friday. I (buy) __________ her a present before then.
5. There isn't any air on the moon. Space colonists (bring) __________ air with them from Earth.
6. I just bought a new camera. I (take) __________ much better pictures with it.

D What do you think the world will be like a hundred years from now? Complete the sentences with your ideas.

1. _______________ might _______________.
2. _______________ may _______________.
3. _______________ could _______________.

First in Space

The first person to travel in space was Yuri Gagarin. He was born in a small village in Russia (in the former Soviet Union) on September 3, 1934. His parents were farmers. He went to work in a steel factory while he was still very young, but he was later chosen to go to a technical high school to study engineering. There, he joined a flying club and learned how to fly small airplanes. At last he knew what he wanted to do with his life.

After he finished his education, he trained to become a military pilot, and he was sent to an air base in the Arctic. The bad weather there made flying extremely difficult, and Gagarin became a highly skilled flyer. In 1960 he was appointed to be in the first group of Soviet astronauts, or *cosmonauts*. Gagarin excelled in this training, because he was very intelligent and also very short. The first spacecraft were very small inside, and Gagarin was only 157 cm (62 inches) tall.

On April 12, 1961, Gagarin became the first person to fly in space in his spacecraft *Vostok 1*. He orbited Earth for 1 hour and 48 minutes. The spacecraft was flown by computers, so during his time in space, he ate and drank, and looked down at our planet for the first time in history. "The Earth is blue," he said, over the radio. "How wonderful. It is amazing." He also sang a patriotic song about Russia. Although he experienced problems with his spacecraft, he landed safely in a farm field.

After his historic flight, Gagarin was a celebrity. He traveled in Italy, Canada, Germany, and Japan and gave lectures about his experience. He desperately wanted to travel in space again, but as a national hero, he was not allowed by the government to risk his life. Instead, he trained other astronauts and pilots. He also worked on a design for a reusable spacecraft, but it was never built. Gagarin died in a flying accident on March 27, 1968. The cause of the accident is still not known.

A Circle **T** for *true* or **F** for *false* or **NI** for *no information* (if the answer is not in the reading).

1.	The first person in space was American.	T	F	NI
2.	Yuri Gagarin learned to fly airplanes as a student.	T	F	NI
3.	Astronauts today are usually very tall.	T	F	NI
4.	Gagarin stayed in space for more than one day.	T	F	NI
5.	*Vostok 1* used computers to fly.	T	F	NI
6.	Gagarin visited other countries to talk about being an astronaut.	T	F	NI
7.	Gagarin flew in space several times.	T	F	NI
8.	Gagarin died after an accident in a spacecraft.	T	F	NI

B Write numbers to put the sentences in chronological order.

____ Gagarin became a military pilot.

____ Gagarin worked in a factory.

____ Gagarin became extremely famous.

____ Gagarin learned to fly.

____ Gagarin was picked to be an astronaut.

____ Gagarin invented a new kind of spacecraft.

____ *Vostok 1* was the first manned mission in space.

C Do you think governments should spend money for space exploration? Give your opinion, and explain your reasons.

____

____

____

____

____

____

____

____

UNIT 12

Review

A Solve the crossword puzzle with vocabulary and grammar from this unit.

Across

2. Earth, Mars, and Jupiter
6. In the future, people _______ live to be 150 years old. It's possible.
9. the planets and the stars (2 words)
11. One of _______, I'm going to clean out all the closets in my house. (2 words)
12. sending people to live in a new place
14. _______ ten years, I will have my own company.
15. Someday _______, we will find a cure for cancer.
16. a vehicle that travels to space

Down

1. _______ day, we will travel to distant stars.
3. Sooner or _______, people will walk on the moon again.
4. a spacecraft people can live on for a short period of time (2 words)
5. I can't swim now. After I take lessons, I will _______ swim. (3 words)
7. I'm going to go out in a little _______.
8. We (go) _______ to Egypt on our vacation next month. (2 words)
9. Today, we use _______ for the weather and communication.
10. The phone is ringing. I _______ answer it.
13. The concert tomorrow _______ at 8 o'clock.

B Circle the correct words to complete the paragraph.

We are used to hearing about (1) (satellites | planets) up in space that can tell us where we are and make our cell phones work. And we know that there is an international (2) (mission | space station) where scientists and astronauts stay and do research. But one of (3) (these | while) days, more tourists will be (4) (going to | able to) choose a trip around the (5) (solar system | orbit) for their vacation as the space tourism industry grows. Space travel companies are looking for more possibilities, and tourists (6) (are going to | might) be able walk on the moon (7) (sooner | one) day!